present perfect

{ 25 Gifts to Sew & Bestow }

betz white

INTER
interw

editor	Leslie T. O'Neill
technical editor	Jacqueline Maxman
illustrations	Missy Shepler
photography	Joe Hancock Swatches by Ann Swanson
photo styling	Pamela Chavez
hair and makeup	Kathy MacKay
art direction	Julia Boyles and Charlene Tiedemann
cover & interior design	Karla Baker
production	Katherine Jackson

Interweave
A division of F+W Media, Inc.
4868 Innovation Drive
Fort Collins, CO 80525
interweave.com

Manufactured in China by RR Donnelley
Shenzhen

Library of Congress
Cataloging-in-Publication Data

White, Betz.
  Present perfect : 25 gifts to sew & bestow / Betz White.
    pages cm
  ISBN 978-1-59668-777-6 (pbk.)
  ISBN 978-1-62033-343-3 (PDF)
1. Machine sewing. 2. Gifts. I. Title.
  TT713.W465 2014
  745.5--dc23
                          2014002434

10 9 8 7 6 5 4 3 2 1

This book is lovingly dedicated to my mom, Janice, who has given me so many gifts. It's my hope that I can be the inspiration to my family that she's been to me.

acknowledgments

I'd like to extend a heartfelt "thank you" to the people who contributed their time and talents to make this book possible. It has been an honor to work with all of you.

To Allison Korleski for her vision and dedication.

To my editor, Leslie O'Neill, for her guidance and encouragement.

To Full Circle Literary and my agent, Stefanie Von Borstel, for her support and expertise.

To all of the fabric suppliers that generously contributed fabrics to the book.

To the women who tested my patterns to help make my instructions more clear.

To Melissa Averinos for her amazing long-arm quilting skills, adding the perfect touch to the Dream Home Quilt and Patchwork Bears Baby Quilt, and to Lucie Summers for her fabulous "porthole" quilt appliqué technique used in the Patchwork Bears Baby Quilt.

To the photographers, Joe Hancock and Ann Swanson, along with stylist Pamela Chavez and hair and makeup artist Kathy MacKay for setting the stage for the projects and creating the beautiful imagery within the book. To Julia Boyles and Charlene Tiedemann for art direction and Karla Baker for the cover and interior design. To Missy Shepler for her detailed illustrations, Jacqueline Maxman for technical editing, and Katherine Jackson for production.

Last, but not least, a very special thank you to my wonderful husband, Dave, and my awesome boys, Conner and Sean. Thank you for your love, support, hugs, and design critiques. Everything I do is better with you!

contents

the gift of *sewing*

When I was a child, my mother sewed many of my clothes, from tops and shorts to matching dresses for me and my doll to Halloween costumes. While at the time I never considered any of these items to be gifts, being sewn for by my mother made me feel special and cared for. She took the time to consider my tastes and to find fabrics and styles that I would love to wear. She showed me that beautiful things can be made rather than bought. Not only that, they were unique and unlike what my friends were wearing. When I became interested in sewing, she taught me how to use her old featherweight machine. Her eagerness to create, be resourceful, and help me learn to sew became a part of who I am.

These lessons were her gift to me, one that I'm honored to share. And what better way to share the gift of sewing than to create a collection of sewing projects for you to stitch and give to those you love? This was my intention behind writing this book, *Present Perfect*.

Make and Give

When designing the projects for *Present Perfect*, I strove for a balance between beauty and usefulness. Pretty things are so much more appreciated when they serve a purpose and fit into our lives with style and function.

Betz wears her guitar recital dress made for her by her mother in 1974.

The twenty-five projects in *Present Perfect* are divided into three collections that cover a wide range of gift-giving situations. Handmade personal accessories are great projects to sew and give for holidays, birthdays, anniversaries, or graduations. The Memorable Milestones chapter has got you covered for those celebrations and virtually any other gift-giving event. From the Wool Courier Bag (page 36) to the Cosmos Infinity Cowl (page 18), you'll find something to make for everyone in your life. Maybe along the way you'll even be inspired to sew one of these projects for yourself. You deserve a gift too, don't you?

The New and Little chapter focuses on babies and kids, offering simple projects for a last-minute shower present, such as the Bib, Rattle & Burp Baby Set (page 76), as well as more elaborate projects with keepsake quality, like the Patchwork Bears Baby Quilt (page 64). Kids are always enjoyable to sew for because there are so many soft fabrics and playful prints available today. Whether you have kids or not, there's a perpetual need for baby gifts.

In the Happy Home chapter you'll find a collection of projects to celebrate a move into a new home and to share with a host or hostess. Settling into a new place can be an exciting yet daunting time. A thoughtful gift such as the Falling Leaves Appliquéd Placemats (page 136) or the Dream Home Quilt (page 144) will provide comfort and calm amid the chaos. And if someone has shown you hospitality, express your gratitude with the Make & Bake Apron (page 108) or the Hot Mitt House & Tea Towel Set (page 124). Either may soon become your go-to hostess gift.

One of a Kind

Sewing gifts lets you create something truly one of a kind. But making the perfect gift takes careful thought and consideration. While your creation can and should be a reflection of your own personality, take a moment to think about the recipient's preferences. Envision his or her personal style, taste, and needs when choosing a project to sew. You can customize a gift by your choice of color and materials. Does the recipient like bold colors or neutral palettes? Does his or her lifestyle require practical fabrics, such as a washable cotton? Or would a fancier silk or wool suit the recipient?

It takes a little bit of matchmaking to combine the personality of the receiver with the perfect gift in the right fabric. For each project I've suggested a material, but feel free to substitute with fabrics that have a similar weight and feel. Throughout this book you'll also find hints for using alternative materials and ideas for upcycling. Reusing a fabric with a history, such as outgrown baby clothing, a grandfather's necktie, or a vintage sheet, can add an additional layer of meaning for a truly memorable gift.

With Love

Receiving a handmade gift feels incredibly special, knowing that it was made with love and care just for you. I've witnessed my own children's excitement build as they've secretly made gifts for one another. It's a joy to see them find such pleasure in creating something that they know their sibling will love.

My hope is that you will thoroughly enjoy making and giving the projects in this book. Think of the recipients and what they mean to you while you're making their gifts. If you have fun with the process, it will most certainly show. And please don't worry about perfection. We are much harder on ourselves than we need to be. Your thoughtful, handmade gift will be received with all of the love and intention that you put into it.

Crafting with Confidence

In this book, there's an achievable gift for all levels of sewers, from the Confident Beginner, who has successfully sewn a few basic projects, to the Eager Intermediate, who's ready for a challenge, to the Seasoned Seamstress, who has seen and sewn it all. With a certain amount of sewing skills, a Confident Beginner can create a gift she's proud to give.

While I advocate letting go of perfection, I also believe in honing our skills to create things that are well crafted with lasting quality. Good craftsmanship is so important, especially for gift giving. It requires patience, practice, and a degree of confidence. Regardless of your experience,

as you work through the projects, you'll pick up a few tips, learn some new techniques, and get lots of good old-fashioned practice. The best part is, the more you sew, the more your confidence will grow!

From choosing the perfect fabric to trimming away the last stray threads, making a gift is deeply gratifying. My goal is for *Present Perfect* to provide you with ideas, inspiration, and information to help you create beautiful, useful things to give your family and loved ones. Sewing itself is a wonderful gift, one that allows you to express your style, creativity, and love through the things you make and give.

stitched with *meaning*

Making a meaningful gift starts with the materials. Finding a fabric in a fantastic print or the most beautiful shade of your friend's favorite color is thrilling when you imagine how much your gift will be appreciated. But beyond aesthetics, the materials you choose can make your gift even more meaningful in other ways.

Organic Fabrics

More than half of the projects in this book are sewn entirely or partially with organic cotton fabrics. That's because I like supporting companies that produce organic fabrics. It makes my heart happy knowing that the fabric I'm using was made without toxic pesticides and with minimal impact on people and the planet.

Although choosing organic isn't always an option, its growing availability, variety, and affordability is making it an easier choice. The environmentally mindful people in your life will be as grateful for your handmade gift as they'll be for your thoughtful use of eco-friendly materials.

Upcycled Materials

Upcycling, recycling, repurposing—whatever you like to call the reuse of materials—is a fun and creative way to find great fabric for your project. Does it seem a little odd to make a gift from a secondhand thing?

Don't think of it as "used." Look at it as a unique, original, and resourceful alternative to buying something new. Reusing vintage items such as boldly printed sheets, kitschy tablecloths, and other items from around your home (or local thrift store) can give a project a playful retro vibe that's truly one of a kind. Giving a gift with a nod to another era can add an endearing quality to your handmade creation.

Well-loved Items

Often people sentimentally hold on to everyday clothing, accessories, or linens that belonged to a family member. These items more often than not stay stored away unseen and unused. Take inspiration from them and the stories they hold by transforming one of them into a cherished gift. A great uncle's necktie repurposed into an eyeglass case, for example, not only makes the tie useful once again but also adds a special layer of meaning.

The Right Stuff

Whether you're scouring a thrift store or the back of your own closet, not everything is suitable for reuse. It's important to select a fabric that is appropriate in weight, hand, and construction for the project you are sewing. Check the fabric for tears, holes, and stains. Some flaws can be worked around, but overall wear and pilling cannot. Generally higher-quality items will last longer and have a better success rate when repurposed.

Consider the end use as well. A delicate silk scarf, for example, would be lovely used as the lining for the Cosmos Infinity Cowl (page 18), yet it would be too fragile to hold up as the lining of the Wool Courier Bag (page 36).

For each project in this book, you'll find a list of materials you'll need to make it along with a fabric suggestion. Many projects also have a "Stitched with Meaning" sidebar with hints for an alternative material that's suitable to repurpose. A few projects, such as those made with wool-blend craft felt, don't have an alternate listed. You'll get the best results for those by sticking to the materials list provided.

I encourage you to use these ideas as a jumping-off point to spark your own creativity. Dig into your stash, your closet, the thrift store, or the fabric store and play with different colors, fabrics, and textures. Gift making can be an expression of yourself, and the more fun you have with it, the more of you will shine through!

things to know
before you sew

Successful sewing requires a bit of forethought, some planning, and a positive attitude. It's always a good idea to read through the full set of instructions, beginning to end, before you start a project. Visualizing the steps ahead of time will help you familiarize yourself with the way the pieces will come together and what you'll need to know to make the project. Please refer to the techniques illustrated on page 154 as they correspond to the project you're sewing.

The degree of difficulty ranges from advanced beginner to experienced. Each project is labeled with a pincushion with one to three pins stuck in it to represent a skill level.

Confident Beginner

You're familiar with your sewing machine and have learned to sew from a class, book, or video. You've successfully sewn a few small projects and are ready to learn more.

Eager Intermediate

You've taken a few sewing classes and have sewn from a sewing pattern. You've completed several projects and are eager to try new techniques.

Seasoned Scamstress

You're a very experienced sewer who has either sewn it all or is ready to try! You are always up for a challenge.

The pattern templates are located in the insert at the back of the book. I suggest making a photocopy or tracing the pattern pieces to keep the originals intact. Be sure to transfer all necessary pattern markings to your traced copy.

For smaller pieces, you might like to trace the templates onto the paper side of a sheet of freezer paper. The freezer paper templates, placed shiny side down, can be lightly fused to the fabric and will stay put while you cut out the pieces. The freezer paper peels away without leaving any residue and can be reused.

Your Sewing Box

Each project calls for a sewing box, which includes your basic sewing necessities. Before you begin to gather the fabrics and notions for your project, make sure you have these standard items on your sewing table:

* Straight pins

* Fabric shears

* Turning tool, such as a chopstick, crochet hook, or knitting needle

* Ruler

* Disappearing-ink fabric marker

* Pencil

* Iron

* Press cloth

* Seam ripper

Best Practices for Sewing

I recommend doing each of these things for most any sewing project (unless the instructions say otherwise). While they are not steadfast rules, I find that practicing these tips will lead to greater sewing success and better craftsmanship.

1   Read through the entire set of instructions before beginning your project.

2   If your project will eventually be washed, prewash and press your fabrics to remove shrinkage.

3   Transfer all pattern markings to your fabrics using a disappearing-ink fabric marker.

4   Backstitch at the beginning and end of every seam.

5   After stitching a seam, clip the corners and intersections of your seam allowances to remove extra bulk in the seams.

6   Clip or notch curved seam allowances to allow seams to lie flat when your work is turned right side out. Clips, or small snips perpendicular to the seam line, are for inner curves. Notches, or wedge-shaped cuts, are for outer curves.

7   Press your seams as you sew for a clean, finished look.

8   Use a press cloth to cover your work when pressing wool, silk, or other delicate fabrics.

9   Don't be afraid to use your seam ripper if you've made a mistake.

10 Trim off stray threads.

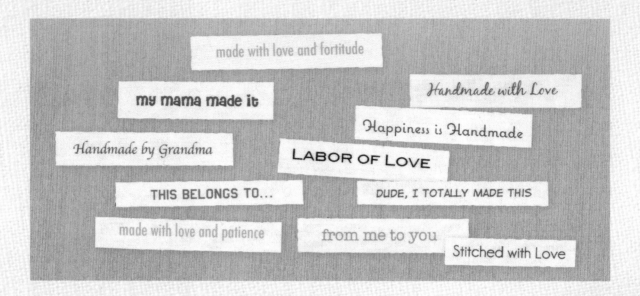

made with love and fortitude

my mama made it

Handmade with Love

Happiness is Handmade

Handmade by Grandma

LABOR OF LOVE

THIS BELONGS TO...

DUDE, I TOTALLY MADE THIS

made with love and patience

from me to you

Stitched with Love

Crafting Handmade Labels

Adding a custom fabric label to a handmade gift is a unique and wonderful way to add a sweet sentiment ("Stitched with Love"), a statement of authorship ("Handmade by Grandma"), or a bit of humor ("Dude, I totally made this"). There are many different ways to create fabric labels. Here are just a few ideas:

* Print onto fabric fused to a sheet of fusible webbing with your inkjet printer.

* Hand embroider with floss on a felt patch.

* Hand write a phrase with a fine-tip permanent-ink fabric marker on fabric.

* Carve a rubber stamp and use textile paint to stamp your message onto fabric.

* Print your message on heat transfer paper, then iron the image onto ribbon or twill tape.

* Print your design on ink-jet printable fabric with your printer.

* Upload your design to Spoonflower.com and order custom-made fabric.

* Order a set of custom printed fabric labels from a seller on Etsy.com.

My favorite technique for making labels is the first choice on the list, using fusible webbing and my inkjet printer at home. The fusible webbing keeps the edges of the label from fraying, and you can simply iron your labels on or sew them to your project. Best of all, you may already have these materials on hand so there is nothing special to buy!

what you'll need

* 1 package of sewable double-sided fusible webbing, such as HeatnBond Lite or Steam-a-Seam

* 1 fat quarter of white cotton sheeting, such as Kona quilting cotton

* Inkjet printer

* Rotary cutter, self-healing mat, and ruler

A Note about Washability

This type of label is best for projects that will require little to no washing, such as a bag or pillow. The ink may fade when laundered. For a more washable label, I prefer to upload my label images to Spoonflower.com. Once you receive your printed fabric, you can apply fusible webbing to the back of the fabric before cutting it into individual labels.

Print Your Own

1 Using a word processing or graphics program on your computer, write whatever words or phrases you'd like to have on your labels. Create a repeat, so several labels will print to an 8.5" × 11" (21.5 × 28 cm) sheet of fused fabric.

Space your labels at least ½" (1.3 cm) apart and do a test print onto paper. Experiment with different colors and fonts. Have fun!

2 Iron your fabric until it's smooth without any wrinkles.

3 Cut an 8.5" × 11" (21.5 × 28 cm) piece of double-sided fusible webbing.

4 Place the "glue" side of the webbing face down onto the wrong side of your fabric with the paper side facing up. Following the manufacturer's instructions, fuse the webbing to the fabric by pressing the paper side of the webbing sheet with an iron. Trim the excess fabric away from the fused edge of the webbing.

5 Adjust your printer settings to accept heavy weight paper. Choose the "high quality" setting for your printing output.

6 If your fabric curls, try to flatten the curl by rolling it in the reverse direction. Manually feed the piece of fused fabric and webbing into the paper feed slot so that the fabric side will be printed on. For most printers, the fabric side should be facing up. Print!

7 Trim apart the labels with a rotary cutter and ruler. Peel the paper backing off of the fused webbing and iron the label in place onto the project. You can add a machine topstitch or zigzag stitch around the edge of the label.

memorable
milestones

Everyone needs to have a few go-to gifts in mind when a special occasion arises. Sewing a handmade gift can help make life's big events even more memorable. This chapter offers eight gift ideas, including bags and accessories, to celebrate birthdays, anniversaries, graduations, and more. And I haven't forgotten about the men in your life! A few projects are designed especially with them in mind.

cosmos infinity
{ cowl }

finished size
9½" × 29½" (24 × 75 cm)

what you'll need

½ yd (45.5 cm) of 60" (152.5 cm) wide cotton jersey for the front

1 yd (91.5 cm) of 45" (114.5 cm) wide woven print cotton for the back

Coordinating thread

Contrasting thread for decorative stitching

Your sewing box

Ballpoint machine needle

Embroidery scissors

Scarves and cowls are such wonderful gifts to give. They are easy to wear, sizing isn't an issue, and you can never have too many! The Cosmos Infinity Cowl is no exception. With a soft cotton jersey on one side and a gorgeous print on the other, the combinations are boundless. You can customize the cowl a step further with some freestyle stitching and reverse-appliqué embellishment. Add as little or as much detail as you wish, but I'm warning you, these techniques are addictive.

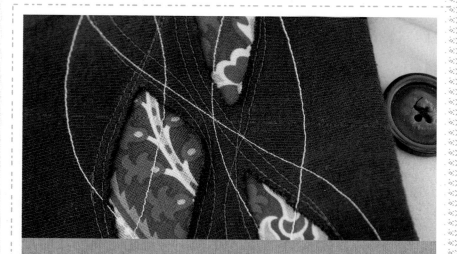

prepare materials

From the cotton jersey, cut:

1 rectangle measuring 10" × 60" (25.5 × 152.5 cm) for the cowl front

From the woven print cotton, cut:

2 rectangles measuring 10" × 30¼" (25.5 × 77 cm) for the cowl back

2 rectangles measuring 5" × 30¼" (12.5 × 77 cm) for the appliqué strip

or

1 rectangle 10" × 60" (25.5 × 152.5 cm) for the cowl back, then skip Step 1

1 rectangle 5" × 60" (12.5 × 152.5 cm) for the appliqué strip, then skip Step 1

Assemble the Panels

1 Layer the two cowl back rectangles right sides together. Sew one set of short ends with a ¼" (6 mm) seam allowance. Press seam open.

Repeat this step with the two appliqué strip rectangles.

2 Place the cowl front on your work surface with the right side down. Layer the appliqué strip, right side down, onto the wrong side of the cowl front, aligning one set of long edges so that the strip is offset to one side **(figure 1)**.

3 Pin the appliqué strip to the wrong side of the cowl front along the edge. Turn the pieces over and pin the other edge of the appliqué strip in place from the right side of the cowl front.

4 With a ruler and a disappearing-ink fabric marker, draw a line 1" (2.5 cm) from the layered edges and another line 4" (10 cm) from the edge. These are the guidelines to stitch between **(figure 2)**.

A Note about Sewing Jersey

This project can be sewn with a straight stitch using a standard foot on a regular sewing machine. However, if you have a walking foot, you may find it useful for sewing on jersey as it will be less likely to stretch as you sew. Using a ballpoint needle allows your needle to slide between the fibers instead of slicing into them, maintaining the integrity of the jersey.

Before you begin sewing the cowl, take time to practice the freehand stitching on scraps first! Sew slowly, taking care to move both layers through the machine evenly.

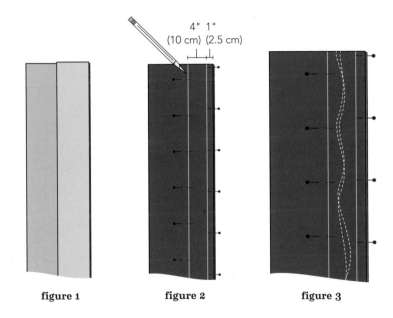

4" (10 cm)   1" (2.5 cm)

figure 1   **figure 2**   **figure 3**

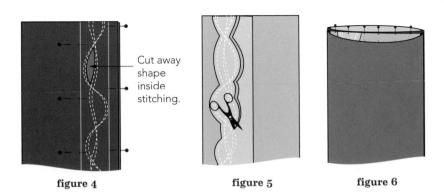

Cut away shape inside stitching.

figure 4   **figure 5**   **figure 6**

Stitch Wavy Lines

5 Using coordinating thread, sew with a straight stitch, starting at one end of the cowl front and stitching between the marked lines. Curve your stitching gradually back and forth, creating long S curves. Sew slowly, taking care to move both layers through the machine evenly.

6 After you stitch the length of the cowl front, sew a second line of stitching loosely following the first (**figure 3**). Then stitch a second set of wavy lines, intersecting with the first set. The shapes created will become the reverse-appliqué areas. If desired, stitch one more set of wavy lines.

Cut Away Shapes

7 Using just the very tips of a pair of sharp, pointed embroidery scissors, snip a tiny hole in the jersey (cowl front only) in the inside of a closed shape created by the waves of stitching. Insert the tip of the scissors and trim away the shape, exposing the appliqué fabric, leaving a ⅛" to ³⁄₁₆" (3 to 5 mm) seam allowance (**figure 4**).

Continue trimming away shapes, first making sure that the area is completely backed with appliqué fabric.

8 Once the desired areas are cut away, change thread to a contrasting color. Add more wavy stitching lines, crossing the newly exposed areas. When you're happy with the decorative stitching, turn the work over so that the wrong side of the cowl front is facing up.

9 With fabric shears, carefully trim away the excess appliqué strip fabric from outside the stitch lines (**figure 5**). Lightly press.

Sew the Cowl

10 Layer the cowl back and front with right sides together. Smooth out the fabric, align, and pin the edges of the long sides. Sew the long sides together with a ¼" (6 mm) seam allowance. Press the seam allowances open, then turn the cowl right side out. Press the seams again.

11 Align the ends of the cowl, with the right sides of the cowl front facing each other. Pin the front ends together and sew with a ¼" (6 mm) seam allowance (**figure 6**).

12 Fold the seam allowances of the cowl back under toward the wrong side and press. Sew closed by hand using the ladder stitch (see Techniques, page 154).

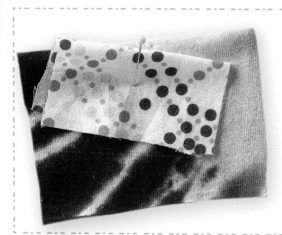

stitched with meaning
turn a well-loved t-shirt into a cozy knit cowl

T-shirts are plentiful, and so is the amount of fabric one XXL T-shirt will yield. Soft, well-loved tees or ones found at the secondhand store are a useful source of cotton jersey. To make the cowl from super-size T-shirts, cut the tees into wide strips, then sew them end to end. Choose a fun fabric to coordinate or upcycle another item of clothing for the lining.

pasha **pleated**

{ clutch }

finished size
6½" × 10½" (16.5 × 26.5 cm)

what you'll need

Pasha Pleated Clutch patterns on side A of the insert

¼ yd (23 cm) or a fat quarter of main fabric

¼ yd (23 cm) or a fat quarter of accent A fabric for pleats

9" × 6" (23 × 15 cm) piece of accent B fabric for flap

¼ yd (23 cm) or a fat quarter of lining fabric

¼ yd (23 cm) of lightweight cotton woven interfacing

Coordinating thread

Coordinating embroidery floss and needle

1 magnetic purse snap, ½"–¾" (1.3–2 cm) in diameter

Your sewing box

Rotary cutter, self-healing mat, and ruler

Handsewing needle

The Pasha Pleated Clutch is the perfect little purse for an evening out or a special event. It's adorned with pretty front pleats and sized just right to hold essentials for the occasion. Make it with coordinating prints, a lustrous sateen, or favorite scraps you've been hanging on to. The Pasha Pleated Clutch makes a cherished gift for bridesmaids, a college graduate, or perhaps even a young girl who would love her own special bag.

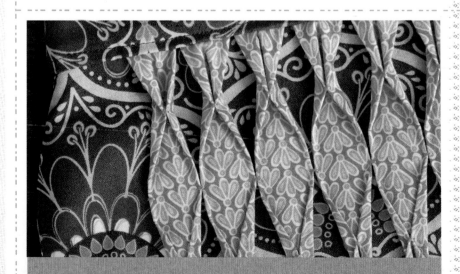

prepare materials

Using the patterns, cut from the main fabric:

1 Front Side Panel

1 reversed Front Side Panel

6 Front Panels

1 Clutch Back

2 Band pieces

Using the pattern, cut from accent A fabric:

7 Pleat pieces

Using the pattern, cut from accent B fabric:

2 Flap pieces

Using the patterns, cut from the lining fabric:

2 Clutch Lining pieces

2 Pocket pieces

Using the patterns, cut from the interfacing:

1 Front Side Panel

1 reversed Front Side Panel

6 Front Panels

1 Clutch Back

2 Band pieces

2 Flap pieces

2 Clutch Lining pieces

Fuse the Interfacing

1 Following the manufacturer's instructions, fuse the interfacing pieces to their respective fabrics. Transfer the pattern markings to the interfaced (wrong) side of your pieces with a disappearing-ink fabric marker.

Make the Clutch Front

2 Fold each Pleat rectangle in half lengthwise, wrong sides together, and press.

3 Place one folded Pleat piece onto the right side of one Front Side Panel. Align the straight edge with the raw edges of the Pleat piece, allowing ½" (1.3 cm) of the Pleat to extend above and below the Front Side Panel. Layer one Front Panel with the right side down and on top, sandwiching the Pleat piece and aligning its top and bottom edges with the Front Side Panel. Pin and sew the long edges together with a ¼" (6 mm) seam allowance **(figure 1)**.

4 Open up that seam and layer another Pleat rectangle onto the right side of the first Front Panel, aligning the edges. Layer a second Front Panel on top of the second Pleat piece. Align the top, bottom, and side edges with the first Front Panel and sew as in Step 3.

5 Continue in this way until all seven Pleat rectangles and six Front Panels are sewn together. End by layering the second Front Side Panel, right sides together, onto the last Front Panel. Align the edges, pin, and sew with a ¼" (6 mm) seam allowance.

6 From the wrong side of the work, press the seam allowances open. From the right side, press each pleat by opening the end and flattening it, so that it is centered on the seam. Repeat until all of the pleats are pressed.

Handstitch the Pleats

7 Using a ruler and a disappearing-ink fabric marker, measure from the top edges of the clutch front and mark three horizontal lines across the pleats at 1½", 3", and 4½" (3.8 cm, 7.5 cm, and 11.5 cm) **(figure 2)**.

8 Starting with the first pleat, bring the folded edges of the pleats together at the upper marking. Bring a needle threaded with one strand of embroidery floss up through the seam under the center of the pleat. Pinch the pleat edges together and make two stitches **(figure 3)**.

Bring the needle back down through the pleat and clutch front under the stitches and tie off at the back of the work, without pulling the stitches tight to the bag.

9 Continue this process for all of the pleats. Do not be tempted to run your stitches

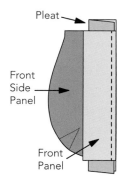

figure 1

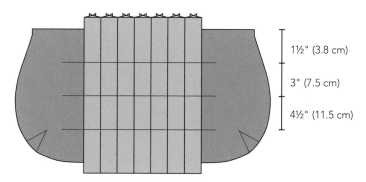

1½" (3.8 cm)

3" (7.5 cm)

4½" (11.5 cm)

figure 2

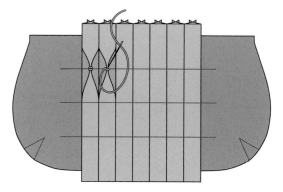

figure 3

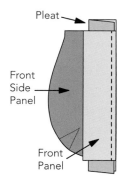

A Note about Pleats

The Pleat rectangles are intentionally cut longer than the Front Side Panels and the Front Panels. This extra fabric allows for the pleats to be handstitched into tucks without distorting the top and bottom edges of the clutch front once it is assembled.

---

together as you move from one pleat to the next. This will pull the pleats together, bunching the clutch front.

Repeat this process again for each pleat at the lowest marking.

10 At the center marking, bring a needle threaded with embroidery floss up through the clutch front where two pleats meet. Stitch the fold of one pleat to another. Make two stitches, then bring the needle back down through the clutch front under the stitches and tie off at the back of the work.

Continue, stitching one pleat to the next. Stitch the first and last pleat to the clutch front.

11 Now that all of the pleats are hand-stitched, use a ruler and a rotary cutter to trim away the excess pleat fabric so that it is flush with the top and the bottom edge of the clutch front. Topstitch the top and bottom ends of the pleats ⅛" (3 mm) from the edge.

Sew the Outer Clutch

12 Beginning with the front of the clutch, match together one set of adjacent dart lines, right sides facing, and pin. Sew along the dart lines, backstitching at the start and stop of the dart.

Match the second set of dart lines, pin, and sew. Trim away any dart fabric on the wrong side at ¼" (6 mm).

Repeat, sewing both darts on the Clutch Back.

13 Layer the front of the clutch and the back, right sides together. Pin sides and bottom, matching the dart seams. Sew together with a ¼" (6 mm) seam allowance, leaving the top edge open. Notch the curved seam allowances, then turn the clutch right side out. Press the sides and bottom seam without flattening the pleats.

Sew the Lining

14 Align the Pocket pieces right sides together and pin. Sew around the perimeter, leaving a 3" (7.5 cm) opening on the bottom edge of each pocket. Snip the seam allowances off at the corners. Turn right side out through the opening, working out the corners with the turning tool. Press, tucking in the seam allowances at the opening.

15 Pin the sewn pocket to the right side of one Clutch Lining piece, centered side to side and 1" (2.5 cm) down from the top edge of the lining. (The unstitched opening from turning the pocket should be at the bottom of the pocket and will be sewn closed in this step.) Edgestitch the pocket sides and bottom, leaving the top open. Backstitch the beginning and end of your sewing to reinforce.

16 Match and sew the darts on the Lining Front and Back as described in Step 12. Pin both lining pieces together, right sides facing, and sew around the sides and bottom edges using a ⅜" (1 cm) seam allowance. Trim the seam allowances to ⅛" (3 mm).

Sew the Flap and Band

17 Following the Flap pattern, mark the placement of the female side of the magnetic snap on the wrong side of one of the Flap pieces.

Install the male component of the snap to one of the Band pieces, according to the pattern marking. (Refer to Techniques, page 154, for instructions on installing the magnetic snap.)

18 Pin both Flap pieces right sides together, aligning the edges. Sew only the curved sides, leaving the straight edge open. Trim the seam allowance to ⅛" (3 mm) and notch the curved seam allowance. Turn right side out, press, and edgestitch.

19 Pin both Band pieces right sides together, aligning the ends. Sew the short ends together with a ¼" (6 mm) seam allowance. Press the seam allowances open and turn right side out.

Assemble the Bag

20 Place the lining into the bag, wrong sides together. Align the side seams and pin the top edges together. Sew together with a ⅛" (3 mm) seam allowance.

21 Place the band inside the lining, right sides together, with the snap toward the bottom and front of the bag. The interior pocket should be on the back of the bag lining. Align the upper edge of the band with the top of the lining and bag, matching all of the side seams.

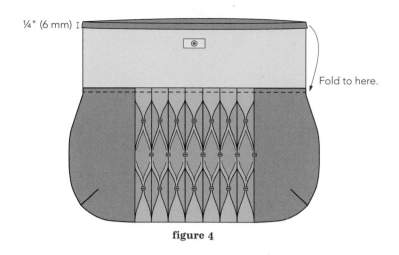

¼" (6 mm) I

Fold to here.

figure 4

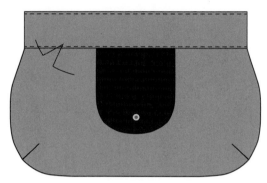

figure 5

Pin and sew together along the top edges using a ¼" (6 mm) seam allowance.

22 Flip the band up and out of the lining and press the seam allowance up toward the band. Press down a ¼" (6 mm) hem at the unsewn edge of the band (**figure 4**).

Fold the band down toward the outside of the bag, just covering the machine stitches at the top of the pleats.

23 At the center back of the bag, insert the straight end of the flap ¼" (6 mm) under the edge of the band, sandwiching it between the band and the clutch back. Make sure the machine stitches are covered and that the flap's snap is facing outward.

Pin the flap and band to the clutch, then edge-stitch at ⅛" (3 mm) along the bottom edge of the band to attach it to the clutch, catching the flap as you sew (**figure 5**).

24 Finish the clutch by edgestitching the top folded edge of the band. Fold the flap to the front and snap.

stitched with meaning
Upcycle a fancy dress into a fashionable clutch

If you've got any "good fabric gone bad"—think prom or bridesmaid dress in a beautiful fabric but unflattering style— consider repurposing part of it into this clutch. A pretty embroidered linen or an intricate damask would be suitable materials, as long as they're not too stiff or bulky.

greta
{ cloche }

finished size

Women's size M: 22"–23" (56–58.5 cm) head circumference

what you'll need

- Greta Cloche patterns on side D of the insert
- ½ yd (45.5 cm) of cotton jersey or other lightweight knit fabric
- 6" × 6" (15 × 15 cm) scraps of wool-blend felt in three different colors
- Coordinating thread
- Your sewing box
- Ballpoint machine needle for sewing knits
- Freezer paper
- Handsewing needle

If I had a nickel for every hat in my closet, I'd have at least a dollar! Hats are great accessories that can really pull an outfit together. The Greta Cloche is easy to wear and fun to make with just a bit of jersey and some scraps of felt. The brim is textured with machine-stitched tucks that create dimension and interest. The felt flowers add just the right pop of color and extra flair. The Greta Cloche is a fabulous easy-fit gift for girlfriends, your mom, or yourself.

prepare materials

Using the pattern, cut from the knit fabric:

2 Cloche Crown pieces

Also cut from the knit fabric:

1 brim measuring 11¼" × 22" (28.5 × 56 cm)

Trace the pattern onto freezer paper, then cut from the felt:

9 Flowers, 3 in each color

Also cut from the felt:

3 strips measuring ¼" × 2" (6 mm × 5 cm), 1 in each color

Trace the Flowers

1 Trace the Flower templates onto the papery side of a piece of freezer paper and loosely cut out each flower. Adhere each template to a piece of felt by placing the shiny side down and lightly pressing on the paper side with a warm, dry iron. Cut out the felt flower along the traced lines, then peel away the freezer paper template.

The templates can be reused to cut out a total of nine flowers: one of each size in three different colors.

Assemble the Crown

2 Fold one Cloche Crown piece along the center mark, right sides together, aligning the edges of the dart, and pin. Sew the dart with a ¼" (6 mm) seam allowance, tapering the seam allowance at the dart point to ⅛" (3 mm). Trim the rest of the seam allowance to ⅛" (3 mm).

Repeat for the second Cloche Crown piece.

3 Layer the two crowns, right sides together, aligning the darts and curved edges. Sew the curved edges with a ¼" (6 mm) seam allowance. Trim the seam allowance to ⅛" (3 mm).

Create the Brim

4 Starting at the bottom edge of the brim piece, measure and mark five parallel lines every 1¼" (3.2 cm) **(figure 1)**. To create tucks, fold the brim piece, wrong sides together, along the first marked line. Sew ¼" (6 mm) from the fold for the entire width of the brim.

Repeat, folding and sewing along the remaining four marked lines.

5 Starting at one end of the brim, measure and mark lines perpendicular to the tucks every 1" (2.5 cm). Following the first line, stitch down the brim over the tucks, making sure they all lay in the same direction.

Repeat this process for every other marked line.

6 Turn your work around and stitch the remaining lines with the tucks pushed in the opposite direction to create an alternating pattern **(figure 2)**.

7 Fold the brim piece in half, right sides together, matching the short ends of the rectangle. Pin, arranging the ends of the tucks up and down, offsetting them from each other. Sew with a ¼" (6 mm) seam allowance. You've now created a circle.

Sew the Cloche

8 Fold the brim lengthwise, wrong sides together, aligning the raw edges.

Now the textured side with the tucks will be referred to as the "right side," and the flat, smooth part of the brim will be referred to as the "wrong side."

9 Fold the brim at the center back seam and mark the opposite fold with a pin as the center front. Match the center front to the center back and mark the folds as the two sides.

10 With the brim wrong side out and the crown right side out, place the crown inside of the brim so that right sides are facing **(figure 3)**. Align and pin the crown side seams with the brim sides along the raw edges. Align and pin the crown center front with the brim center front along the raw edges.

Repeat for the two center back markings.

A Note about Grain

When you're cutting the brim from the knit fabric, make sure the grain runs with the height of the brim and the stretch runs across the width.

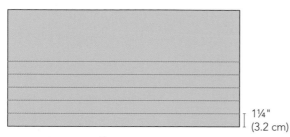

1¼"
(3.2 cm)

figure 1

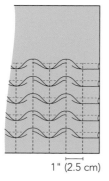

1" (2.5 cm)

figure 2

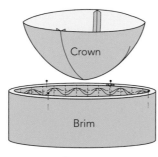

Crown

Brim

figure 3

Side
Crown
Back
Front
Side
Brim

figure 4

Distribute the rest of the fabric in between the pins evenly, pinning raw edges together **(figure 4)**. Sew the brim to the crown with a ¼" (6 mm) seam allowance. Turn right side out.

Create the Felt Flowers

11 With coordinating thread, fold each petal in half vertically and make small whip-stitches (see Techniques, page 154) along the back to create dimension.

Repeat this for each flower shape and petal.

12 Stack the flowers into three sets, small to large, alternating colors. Tie a knot in the center of each of the felt strips to create a flower center. Place one knot in the center of each flower set.

13 Handsew each flower set together with a needle and thread. Double thread the needle and knot the thread. Come up from the back of the large flower, stitching through all three flower layers and the felt knot in the center. Continue to stitch until the layers are secure.

14 Place the three sewn flower sets onto the side of the brim. Pin in desired position and hand-tack the flowers to the brim with needle and thread.

stitched with meaning
transform a cast-off sweater into a felted cloche

When your prettiest fine-gauge sweater or jersey T-shirt suffers a disaster, give it a second chance as a classy cloche. Check it carefully for wear or pilling before cutting out the pieces and only use fabric that will shine in its new life as an accessory.

While you're repurposing, make the flowers out of felted wool from a cast-off sweater. Wash a 90% to 100% wool (or wool blended with other animal fibers) garment in hot water with detergent. Air or machine dry to create thick, dense felt that won't fray when cut.

eye candy
{ glasses case }

what you'll need

Eye Candy Glasses Case patterns on side A of the insert

8" × 8" (20.5 × 20.5 cm) square of fabric A, a light- to medium-weight woven

8" × 8" (20.5 × 20.5 cm) square of fabric B, a light- to medium-weight woven

12" × 12" (30.5 × 30.5 cm) square of lining fabric

12" × 12" (30.5 × 30.5 cm) square of interfacing

12" × 12" (30.5 × 30.5 cm) square of fusible fleece or batting

Coordinating thread

1½" (3.8 cm) of 1" (2.5 cm) wide grosgrain ribbon

1 magnetic snap, ¾" (2 cm) in diameter

Your sewing box

Pinking shears

Zipper foot for your sewing machine (optional)

Everybody needs a handy place to stash eyeglasses, readers, or shades. As a newbie to glasses myself, the whereabouts of my eyewear is often unknown. Without a safe place to keep them, mine are lost if they're not sitting on my nose! Here comes the Eye Candy Glasses Case to the rescue. Fun and functional, the case is softly padded and has a magnetic snap and flap closure. Sew it up with eye-catching fabrics so you'll be sure to spot your specs even in the bottom of your bag. Give the Eye Candy Glasses Case with a hot new paperback to your book club hostess or favorite teacher.

prepare materials

Using the patterns, cut from fabric A and interfacing:

1 Side Front

1 reversed Side Front

1 Side Back/Flap

1 reversed Side Back/Flap

Using the patterns, cut from fabric B and interfacing:

1 Center Front

1 Center Back/Flap

Using the patterns, cut from the lining fabric and fusible fleece:

1 Front Lining piece

1 Back/Flap Lining piece

Fuse the Interfacing

1 Fuse the interfacing or fusible fleece pieces to their respective fabrics. Transfer the pattern markings to the wrong side (on the fleece or interfacing) of your pieces with a disappearing-ink fabric marker.

Sew the Front Pieces

2 Align one side edge of the Center Front piece to the edge of one Side Front piece, placing right sides together. Sew with a ¼" (6 mm) seam allowance, then press the seam open.

Repeat, sewing the reversed Side Front piece to the other edge of the Center Front piece.

3 Topstitch both seams ⅛" (3 mm) from the seam line on both of the Side Front pieces **(figure 1)**.

4 Align one side edge of the Center Back/Flap piece to the edge of one Side Back/Flap piece, placing right sides together. Sew with a ¼" (6 mm) seam allowance, then press the seam open.

Repeat, sewing the reversed Center Back/Flap piece to the other edge of the Side Back/Flap piece.

5 Topstitch both seams ⅛" (3 mm) from the seam line on both of the Side Back/Flap pieces **(figure 2)**.

6 Start with the sewn front panel of the glasses case, oriented wrong side up. Match together one set of adjacent dart lines. Sew along the dart lines, backstitching at the start and stop of the dart. Match the second set of dart lines, pin, and sew.

Repeat for the Front Lining piece.

Install the Snap

7 Fuse a small piece (1" × 2" [2.5 × 5 cm]) of fusible fleece to the wrong side of the front of the case, surrounding the snap placement area. This will provide reinforcement for the snap. Transfer the marking for the snap placement to the interfacing. (Refer to Techniques, page 154, for magnetic snap installation tips.)

8 Repeat Step 7 to install the opposite component of the snap on the right side of the case flap's lining. Mark the snap placement on the wrong side (the fusible fleece).

9 With right sides together, pin the front panel to the back and flap of the case, aligning the front dart seams with the pattern markings on the back and flap. Sew together with a ¼" (6 mm) seam allowance. Trim the seam allowances with pinking shears to ³⁄₁₆" (5 mm).

Repeat this step to sew the lining front and back and flap. Leave a 3" (7.5 cm) opening along the bottom edge for turning.

Assemble the Case

10 Fold the 1½" (3.8 cm) length of grosgrain ribbon in half, matching the cut ends. Sew ends together with a ¼" (6 mm) seam allowance.

11 Find the center point of the outer flap. Pin the ribbon so that it is centered and

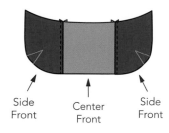

Side Front   Center Front   Side Front

figure 1

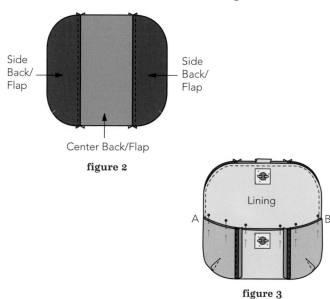

Side Back/ Flap   Side Back/ Flap

Center Back/Flap

figure 2

Lining

A   B

figure 3

the stitch line of the ribbon is aligned with the edge of the flap. The fold of the ribbon should be pointing away from the edge and toward the back of the case.

12 With right sides facing, slide the lining inside the exterior case. Align and pin all of the flap and front edges. Sew around the flap with a ¼" (6 mm) seam allowance, starting at the side seam at the top of the case front (A), and stopping at the other side seam at the top of the front (B) **(figure 3)**.

13 Move the seam allowances out of the way, then sew the top edge of the front from one seam to the other (from B to A). Trim the curves of the seam allowance with pinking shears. Clip and trim the seam allowances where the front meets the back.

14 Turn work right side out through the lining opening, working out the curved seams with your fingers to be sure they are fully turned. Press. Turn in the seam allowances of the 3" (7.5 cm) opening in the lining, press, and topstitch or handsew the opening closed.

15 Push the lining down inside the outer case. Topstitch around the perimeter for the case opening, ⅛" (3 mm) from the edge. Use the zipper foot attachment on your machine if the snaps get in the way of the standard foot.

stitched with meaning
re-style dad's favorite tie into a handy case

Smaller projects, such as this eyeglass case, can be made from smaller items, such as neckties. Necktie fabric is usually silk, and many have tiny patterns and details that are fun to reuse in a different type of accessory. Often people have sentimental feelings about old neckties that belonged to family members, so giving a gift made from one will make it extra special.

wool courier { bag }

finished size
10" × 14" × 2½"
(25.5 × 35.5 × 6.5 cm)

what you'll need
Wool Courier Bag patterns on side B of the insert

½ yd (45.5 cm) of 36" (91.5 cm) wide wool-blend felt for the body

½ yd (45.5 cm) of 54" (137 cm) wide plaid wool suiting for the flap and accents

½ yd (45.5 cm) of 45" (114.5 cm) wide lining

1 yd of 20" (51 cm) wide woven cotton fusible interfacing

½ yd (45.5 cm) of 45" (114.5 cm) wide fusible fleece

2½" × 18" (6.5 × 45.5 cm) piece of heavy-duty stabilizer

Coordinating thread

1 magnetic snap, ½"–¾" (1.3–2 cm) in diameter

Three 1½" (3.8 cm) wide rectangular metal rings

One 1½" (3.8 cm) wide metal slider buckle

Your sewing box

Zipper foot for your sewing machine

The Wool Courier Bag is an old-school solution to carrying your modern stuff with style. Messenger-type bags have been around since the Pony Express and have become a classic carryall for both genders. Roomy but not cumbersome, the Wool Courier Bag has pockets inside and out, a magnetic snap closure, and an adjustable strap. The combination of felt and wool plaid makes this bag not only handsome to look at but also satisfying to sew. Stitch one up for someone heading back to school, commuting to a new job, or taking on another of life's adventures.

prepare materials

Using the patterns, cut from the wool-blend felt:

2 Bag Front/Bag Back pieces

2 Side Gussets

1 Back Pocket

1 Snap Tab

Also cut from the wool-blend felt:

1 flap accent strip measuring 1½" × 12" (3.8 × 30.5 cm)

Using the patterns, cut from the plaid wool suiting:

1 Bag Flap

4 Corner Patches

2 Strap Loops

Also cut from the plaid wool suiting:

1 strap measuring 3½" × 54" (9 × 137 cm)

1 bottom gusset measuring 3" × 18½" (7.5 × 47 cm)

Using the patterns, cut from the lining:

2 Bag Front/Bag Back pieces

1 Bag Flap

2 Lining Pockets

1 Back Pocket

4 Corner Patches

Also cut from the lining:

1 lining gusset measuring 3" × 33" (7.5 × 84 cm)

Using the patterns, cut from the fusible interfacing:

2 Bag Front/Bag Back pieces

2 Side Gussets

1 Snap Tab

1 Bag Flap

1 Back Pocket

Also cut from the fusible interfacing:

1 strap measuring 1½" × 54" (3.8 × 137 cm)

1 bottom gusset measuring 3" × 18½" (7.5 × 47 cm)

Using the patterns, cut from the fusible fleece:

2 Front Bag/Back Bag pieces

1 Bag Flap

1 Lining Pocket

Also cut from the fusible fleece:

1 lining gusset measuring 3" × 33" (7.5 × 84 cm)

1 square measuring 1" × 1" (2.5 × 2.5 cm) for the snap reinforcement

Cut from the heavy-duty stabilizer:

1 bottom gusset measuring 2½" × 18" (6.5 × 45.5 cm)

Fuse the Interfacing

1 Following the manufacturer's instructions, fuse the interfacing pieces to the wrong sides of these wool-blend felt and plaid wool pieces: two Bag Front/Bag Back pieces, two Side Gussets, one Back Pocket, and one Bag Flap.

For the bottom gusset, center and sandwich the piece of heavy-duty stabilizer between the wrong side of the suiting and the interfacing, and then fuse the interfacing. For the strap, fuse the interfacing onto one half of the wrong side. For the Snap Tab, trim the interfacing down ¼" (6 mm) on each side, center, and fuse to the wrong side of the Snap Tab piece.

2 Following the manufacturer's instructions, fuse the fleece pieces to the wrong sides of these lining pieces: two Bag Front/Bag Back pieces, one Bag Flap, one Lining Pocket, and the lining gusset rectangle.

3 Separate the Bag Front/Bag Back pieces cut from the wool-blend felt and the lining. Make two sets, one for the front and the other for the back. Work with each set separately.

Sew the Lining

4 Place two Lining Pocket pieces right sides together. Sew across the top edge with a ¼" (6 mm) seam allowance. Turn right sides out and press the seam.

Topstitch the seam ¼" (6 mm) from the edge.

5 Lay the sewn pocket on top of the Back Bag lining piece, right sides up. Align, pin, and sew the bottom and side edges with a ⅛" (3 mm) seam allowance.

6 Measure and mark vertical lines from the top edge of the pocket, using a disappearing-ink fabric marker, at 2" and 4" (5 cm and 10 cm) from the right edge. Sew through all layers at these marks, perpendicularly from the top edge of the pocket, to create pocket segments.

7 Find and mark the center point of the lining gusset and of the Bag Front and Bag Back lining pieces.

8 Pin the lining gusset to the edge of the Back Bag lining, right sides together, aligning the center points. Pin along the sides and bottom, distributing the fabric evenly. Sew together with a ⅜" (1 cm) seam allowance.

9 Pin the Bag Front lining piece to the lining gusset, matching center markings and distributing the fabric evenly, and sew with a ⅜" (1 cm) seam allowance. Leave a 5" (12.5 cm) opening along the bottom edge for turning. Trim seam allowances to ³⁄₁₆" (5 mm).

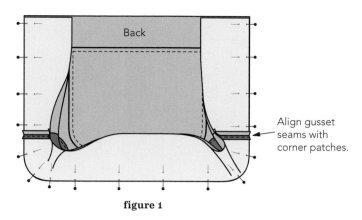

Back

Align gusset seams with corner patches.

figure 1

A Note about Wool Plaid

When you work with fabrics like a woven plaid, it is especially important to be aware of the grain line when cutting out your pieces. Aligning the pattern pieces on grain—that is, with the marked grain line parallel to the fabric's selvedge—will assure that the plaid will be straight on your project.

When working with wool, use a press cloth to protect your fabric.

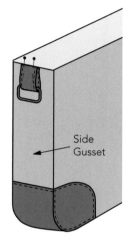

Side Gusset

figure 2

Sew the Outer Bag

10 Place a plaid Corner Patch and a lining Corner Patch right sides together. Align them and sew one side from point to point with a ¼" (6 mm) seam allowance. Trim and notch the seam allowances, turn right side out, and press.

Repeat this process for the three other patches.

11 Place one sewn Corner Patch on the right side of the Bag Front piece, aligning the raw edges with the bottom edge of the corner. Pin and edgestitch all sides of the Corner Patch to the Bag Front ⅛" (3 mm) from the edge.

Repeat this process, sewing the other sewn Corner Patch to the Bag Front and the remaining two Corner Patches to the Bag Back piece.

12 Install the female side of the magnetic snap to the Bag Front, following the placement mark on the pattern. (Refer to instructions for installing magnetic snaps on page 154).

13 Layer the felt Back Pocket piece with the Back Pocket lining, right sides together, and pin. Sew around the perimeter with a ¼" (6 mm) seam allowance, leaving a 3" (7.5 cm) opening in one side to turn the work. Clip corners and notch the curved seam allowances.

Turn right side out and press. Work out the corners with a turning tool and fold in the seam allowance at the opening. Topstitch across the top edge of the pocket ¼" (6 mm) from the edge.

14 Place the sewn back pocket right side up onto the right side of the felt Bag Back piece, 2" (5 cm) down from the top edge and centered side to side.

Pin and topstitch the back pocket around the sides and bottom ¼" (6 mm) from the edge, closing the side opening. Backstitch at the beginning and end to reinforce the top edge of the pocket.

15 Layer one Side Gusset piece on top of the bottom gusset, right sides together, and align the short ends. Sew with a ¼" (6 mm) seam allowance. Press the seam open. Edgestitch the bottom gusset ⅛" (3 mm) from the seam.

Repeat this process for the second Side Gusset, sewing it to the other end of the bottom gusset.

16 Pin the sewn side gusset to the side and bottom edges of the Bag Back piece, taking care to align the gusset seams with the top of the corner patches. Sew the entire gusset to the Bag Back with a ¼" (6 mm) seam allowance **(figure 1)**.

Repeat this process, sewing the Bag Front to the gusset. Trim seam allowances to ³⁄₁₆" (5 mm) and notch the curved seam allowances. Press seams.

17 Fold one Strap Loop piece crosswise in half, right sides together. It should measure 1½" × 3" (3.8 × 7.5 cm) when folded.

Sew the longer edges together with a ¼" (6 mm) seam allowance. Turn right side out and press. Edgestitch the seam and folded edge at ⅛" (3 mm).

18 Thread a rectangular ring onto the Strap Loop and fold it in half. Pin the raw edges of the loop to the top edge of the Side Gusset piece, centering it with the loop hanging down. Sew it to the gusset with a ⅛" (3 mm) seam allowance (**figure 2**, page 39).

Repeat this process for the second Strap Loop.

Sew the Flap

19 Layer the plaid Bag Flap piece on top of the Bag Flap lining piece, right sides together. Sew the sides and the bottom edge together with a ¼" (6 mm) seam allowance. Leave the straight edge at the top unsewn.

Trim the seam allowances and notch the curves. Turn right side out and press. Topstitch the sides and bottom edge of the flap ¼" (6 mm) from the edge.

20 Center the flap accent strip down the center front of the bag flap, starting at the top raw edge. Allow the excess length of the accent strip to hang off at the bottom edge. Pin, then edgestitch down one side of the accent strip at ⅛" (3 mm), stitching past the bottom edge of the flap for the entire length of the strip.

Repeat, edgestitching down the other edge of the accent strip in the same manner.

21 Thread the loose end of the accent strip through a rectangular ring, then fold it back to the lining side of the flap and pin. From the front of the flap, topstitch a 1" (2.5 cm) square with an X in the center at the end of the strip through all of the layers. Trim any excess strip from the lining side of the flap.

22 Edgestitch both long edges of the Snap Tab piece at ⅛" (3 mm). Stitch a 1" (2.5 cm) square with an X in the center 1¾" (4.5 cm) above the bottom end of the tab.

23 Fuse the 1" (2.5 cm) square of fusible fleece on top of the interfacing below the X. Install the male side of the magnetic snap so that the snap is on the right side of the tab and the washer is on the fusible fleece, ¾" (2 cm) up from the end (**figure 3**).

24 Fold the end of the Snap Tab toward the wrong side of the tab so that the snap is on the back of the X. Using a zipper foot, stitch over the previous edgestitching on either side of the snap (**figure 4**).

Thread the other end of the tab through the rectangular ring on the flap. Topstitch across

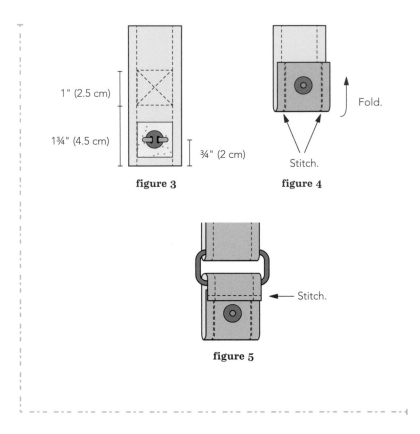

1" (2.5 cm)

1¾" (4.5 cm)

¾" (2 cm)

figure 3

Fold.

Stitch.

figure 4

Stitch.

figure 5

the tab at the overlap, catching all layers. Trim excess from the back (**figure 5**).

25 Place the flap onto the Bag Back piece, right sides facing. Align, pin, and sew the top edge of the flap to the top edge of the Bag Back with a ⅛" (3 mm) seam allowance.

Attach the Lining

26 Place the outer bag inside the bag lining, right sides together. The Back Pocket lining piece should be facing the flap.

Pin the top edge of the outer bag and the bag lining, taking care to align all of the side seams, sandwiching the flap edge and the strap loops. Carefully sew together with a ¼" (6 mm) seam allowance. Trim the seam allowances at intersections to reduce extra bulk.

27 Carefully reach into the opening in the bottom seam of the lining and pull the outer bag through the opening. Turn the lining right side out. Fold in the seam allowances at

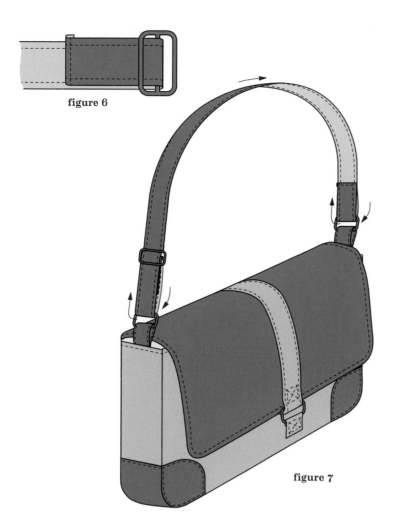

figure 6

figure 7

the opening in the lining and close them by topstitching at ⅛" (3 mm).

28 Push the lining down inside the outer bag and carefully press the top seam. Topstitch through all layers around the top edge of the bag at ¼" (6 mm).

Sew the Strap

29 Fold the strap in half lengthwise, right sides together. Sew the sides together with a ¼" (6 mm) seam allowance. Turn right side out through one end with a turning tool and press the seam to one side. Edgestitch the seam and folded edge at ⅛" (3 mm).

30 Thread the end of the strap through the rectangular buckle and over the center bar. Fold the end of the strap under ¼" (6 mm) and stitch to the strap about 3" (7.5 cm) away from the buckle (figure 6).

31 Thread the other end of the strap through one of the rectangular rings attached to the bag. Lace the end through the buckle then through the other rectangular ring at the opposite side of the bag. Fold the end of the strap under ¼" (6 mm) and stitch to the strap about 3" (7.5 cm) away from the ring (figure 7).

stitched with meaning
upcycle a thrifted wool suit into a hip new bag

Sometimes a moth will end the life of a suit before its time. Consider repurposing the good fabric into the flap and other details of the Wool Courier Bag. Toss the suit into the dryer for fifteen minutes to eliminate any remaining wool eaters first. You may need to piece the fabric together to work around holes and seams, but that will just add a little more character to the bag.

coffee cash
{ coin pouch }

finished size
3½" × 4½" (9 × 11.5 cm)

what you'll need

Coffee Cash Coin Pouch patterns on side C of the insert

8" × 10" (20.5 × 25.5 cm) piece of white medium-weight twill or canvas main fabric

8" × 10" (20.5 × 25.5 cm) piece of lining fabric

5" × 5" (12.5 × 12.5 cm) square of brown wool-blend felt

Coordinating thread

One 3½" (9 cm) flex coin-purse frame

1 quarter or other coin

Your sewing box

Pinking or other decorative shears (optional)

Sharp needle (optional)

Embroidery floss in two colors and needle (optional)

Pliers (optional)

Change is good! Especially when you corral it in something as cute and functional as the Coffee Cash Coin Pouch. This cup-shaped pouch has an easy-to-install flex frame closure that pops open when you give the sides a squeeze. Toss your change in today and have it handy the next time you order your favorite mocha-latte-chino-frappé! Make one as a super gift for your highly caffeinated friend and, as an extra bonus, tuck in a gift card for her local café.

prepare materials

Using the pattern, cut from the main fabric and the lining:
2 Coffee Cash Cup pieces

Using the pattern, cut from the felt:
2 Coffee Cash Bands

figure 1

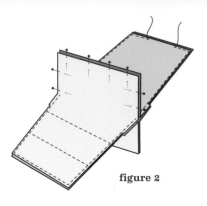

figure 2

Assemble the Pouch

1 Use decorative shears to cut the top and bottom edges of the Coffee Cash Band pieces, if desired. Transfer pattern markings to fabrics with a disappearing-ink fabric marker.

2 Embellish the felt Coffee Cash Band pieces with appliqué or embroidery if desired. The sidebar explains how to do shisha embroidery with a coin, as shown in the photo.

3 Layer one Band onto the right side of one of the Coffee Cash Cup pieces cut from the main fabric, following the pattern markings, and pin. Topstitch across the top and bottom edge of the Band ⅛" (3 mm) from the edge.

Repeat for the second Band and Coffee Cash Cup piece cut from the main fabric.

4 Layer both Coffee Cash Cup pieces right sides together, sandwiching the Bands, and pin the side edges. Sew with a ¼" (6 mm) seam allowance from the upper flap marking down one side of the cup, across the bottom, and up the other side to the second flap marking **(figure 1)**.

5 Repeat for the two Coffee Cash Cup lining pieces, leaving a 1½" (3.8 cm) opening along the bottom for turning. Trim the seam allowances to ⅛" (3 mm), starting and stopping ¼" (6 mm) away from the pattern markings.

6 Following the pattern markings, separate the cup flaps. Align and pin one outer cup flap to one lining cup flap, right sides together. Begin sewing where the stitching from Step 4 ends and sew around the flap with a ¼" (6 mm) seam allowance to where the stitching begins again. Sew through only two layers **(figure 2)**.

Repeat, sewing the other outer cup flap and lining cup flap together. Trim the flap seam allowances and clip corners.

7 Turn the work right side out through the hole in the lining. Work out all of the corners with a turning tool. Fold in the seam allowance at the bottom of the lining and topstitch the opening closed at ¹⁄₁₆" (2 mm) from the fold. Push the lining down inside the outer cup. Press, making sure the corners of the flaps are square.

Create Casings and Install the Frame

8 Fold one flap down toward the outside of the pouch, aligning the flap edge with the upper pattern marking. Sew across the flap ⅛" (3 mm) from the edge, using a backstitch at the beginning and end of the seam to secure **(figure 3)**. This creates a casing for the frame.

Repeat, creating a casing with the second flap. Topstitch the folded top edge of each flap ⅛" (3 mm) from the edge.

9 Thread each piece of the flex frame through the open ends of the casings **(figure 4)**. Line up a set of hinges at one end and slide the metal pin through the hinge. Squeeze with pliers to secure if necessary **(figure 5)**.

Repeat for the second hinge at the other end of the casings.

10 If desired, handsew the ends of the casing together with a ladder stitch (see Techniques, page 154) to conceal the hinges.

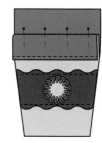

figure 3

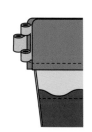

figure 4

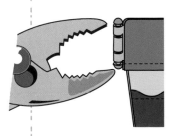

figure 5

Indian Shisha Embroidery How-to

Shisha, or mirror work, embroidery attaches small pieces of mirrors to fabric. For the Coffee Cash Coin Pouch, you attach a quarter instead! Basic embroidery stitches surround the coin, creating a border that holds the coin flush to the fabric.

1 Thread a sharp needle with embroidery floss. Hold a quarter on the surface of the fabric with your thumb. Refer to Techniques, page 154, for tips on making these embroidery stitches.

To make the foundation stitches, bring the needle up through the back of the work at the bottom of the quarter left of center. Bring the needle back down through the fabric at the top of the quarter, making a vertical stitch across the coin.

Make a second stitch horizontally across the coin to the right of center. Repeat, making four stitches across the coin like a hashtag or number sign (#) **(figure 1)**.

2 Make a second set of foundation stitches at a 45-degree angle from the first set **(figure 2)**.

3 Bring your needle up at the bottom of the coin. Next, slide your needle under the foundation stitches from the center toward the edge **(figure 3)**. Pull the needle through to tighten up the stitch. Work one backstitch right next to the coin **(figure 4)**.

4 Repeat, threading your needle under the foundation stitches from the center toward the edge. Make sure your thread is looped under the needle as you pull your stitch tight, similar to the blanket stitch **(figure 5)**. As you work the backstitch after your blanket stitch, be sure to bring the needle down through the previous backstitch. Continue working these two stitches around the coin.

As you work around the coin, the foundation stitches will be pulled toward the outer edge, creating a secure frame around the coin.

You can add a second border using the chain stitch in a second floss color, as shown in the photograph.

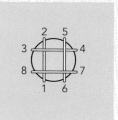

figure 1

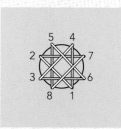

figure 2

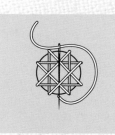

figure 3

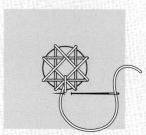

figure 4

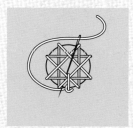

figure 5

cargo
{ tablet sleeve }

finished size

The interior measures 7¾" × 9½" (19.5 × 24 cm) and fits most iPad tablets. Check the dimensions of your tablet or e-reader and enlarge or reduce the patterns if necessary.

what you'll need

Cargo Tablet Sleeve patterns on side A of the insert

⅓ yd (30.5 cm) of waxed canvas or other mid-weight canvas or twill for the exterior

⅓ yd (30.5 cm) of lining fabric

⅓ yd (30.5 cm) of fleece batting

9" (23 cm) length of 1" (2.5 cm) wide nylon webbing

Coordinating thread

1" (2.5 cm) side-release buckle or 1" (2.5 cm) D ring and 1" (2.5 cm) swivel clip

Your sewing box

Zipper foot for your sewing machine

Clover Wonder Clips or paper clips

Heavy duty needle for your sewing machine (optional)

Seems almost everyone has some kind of tablet or e-reader and a need for something to keep it in. The Cargo Tablet Sleeve will protect a device from dust, moisture, and scratches. Made in a waxed canvas fabric, which was first used as sailcloth by nineteenth-century mariners, the tablet sleeve is durable and has a look similar to distressed leather. Adding a strip of webbing with a buckle closure is a snap and will give a high-tech tablet an old-school feel.

prepare materials

Using the patterns, cut from the main fabric:

2 Upper Front/Back pieces

2 Lower Front/Back pieces

1 Flap

Using the patterns, cut from the lining fabric and the fleece batting:

2 Interior pieces

1 Flap

From the webbing, cut:

1 length measuring 3" (7.5 cm) for the lower strap

1 length measuring 6" (15 cm) for the flap strap

A Note about Materials

Waxed canvas is a type of canvas that is impregnated with wax and is water resistant. It has a slightly waxy feel and gets a rugged, mottled look with use. Waxed canvas can be pressed, provided you protect your iron from the wax with a press cloth. The seams can be finger pressed by using the heat and pressure from your hands to smooth and flatten them. Sometimes when pinning waxed canvas, pinholes can show, so try to pin carefully within the seam allowances. If you're comfortable sewing without pins, forgo them and use Clover Wonder Clips or paper clips instead.

Waxed canvas can be difficult to find because there are very few manufacturers still producing it. Try searching for it in "supplies" on Etsy.com for small quantities. For larger quantities, see Resources (page 158) for suppliers.

Nylon webbing can be finished easily by singeing the cut ends with a lighted match. Carefully move the tip of the flame back and forth across the end of the webbing just until the fibers fuse. Allow the end to cool before touching.

Sew the Exterior

1 Place the Lower Back piece on top of the Upper Back piece, right sides together, aligning the bottom edges. Sew together with a ¼" (6 mm) seam allowance.

Finger press the seam open. Topstitch ⅛" (3 mm) from the seam on the Lower Back piece.

2 Layer and pin one end of the 3" (7.5 cm) length of webbing onto the right side of the Lower Front piece, centering it on the template marking. Sew together ⅛" (3 mm) from the edge **(figure 1)**.

3 Place the Lower Front piece on top of the Upper Front piece, right sides together, sandwiching the webbing and aligning the bottom edges. Sew together with a ¼" (6 mm) seam allowance **(figure 2)**.

Finger press the seam open, then topstitch ⅛" (3 mm) from that seam on the Lower Front piece.

4 Thread the end of the webbing through the outer component to the side release buckle (or D ring) and tuck the end back under itself at the seam line **(figure 3)**. Topstitch a 1" (2.5 cm) square and an X through both layers of the webbing and the Upper Front piece to secure. Using

a zipper foot may help you maneuver more closely to the buckle.

5 Place the front exterior and the back exterior panels right sides together, aligning the side and bottom edges and matching the ends of the lower seams. Pin, then sew the sides and bottom edges together with a ¼" (6 mm) seam allowance.

6 Trim the seam allowances to ⅛" (3 mm), clip the corners, and then turn the work right side out. Work out the corners with a turning tool and finger press the seams flat or use an iron and a press cloth.

Sew the Lining and Flap

7 Layer the Interior batting pieces onto the wrong sides of the Interior lining pieces. Place them right sides together, so that the lining pieces are sandwiched in between the batting. Pin the side and bottom edges, then sew with a ¼" (6 mm) seam allowance. Trim the seam allowances to ⅛" (3 mm) and clip the corners.

8 Layer the flap components, starting with the Flap batting, then the Flap lining, right sides up. Next, layer and pin one end of the 6"

figure 1

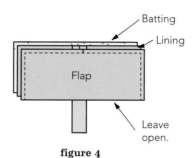

figure 2

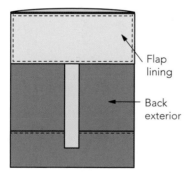

Tuck end under and topstitch.

figure 3

Batting

Lining

Flap

Leave open.

figure 4

Flap lining

Back exterior

figure 5

(15 cm) length of webbing onto the right side of the Flap lining, centering it as shown on the pattern. Last, layer the main fabric Flap piece, right side down. Pin the side and front edges, then sew with a ¼" (6 mm) seam allowance (**figure 4**).

9 Trim the seam allowances to ⅛" (3 mm), clip the corners, and then turn right side out. Work out the corners with a turning tool, then finger press the seams flat.

10 Topstitch the side and front edges at ⅛" (3 mm).

11 Align the unsewn edge of the flap with the top edge of the back exterior, right sides facing. Sew together with a ¼" (6 mm) seam allowance (**figure 5**).

12 Thread the end of the flap webbing through the inner component of the side release buckle (or the loop of the swivel clip) and fold the end back under itself. Clip the hardware together. Adjust the webbing to the desired length, then secure with a pin and unclip the hardware.

13 Topstitch a 1" (2.5 cm) square with an X through both layers of the webbing. A zipper foot might also make this step easier to complete. Trim the excess webbing if necessary.

Assemble the Sleeve

14 Slide the lining, wrong side out, into the exterior, which is right side out. Work the corners of the lining into the exterior corners, smooth the layers, and align the top edges and side seams.

15 Fold a ¼" (6 mm) hem of the exterior and the flap seam allowance toward the wrong side and finger press. Fold a ¼" (6 mm) hem of the interior and batting toward the wrong side. Align the folded edges, securing with Clover Wonder Clips or paper clips.

16 Topstitch the interior and exterior together ⅛" (3 mm) from the top.

gentleman's

{ travel case }

Good grooming requires effort, but even more importantly, it takes the right tools and supplies. The Gentleman's Travel Case is ready to assist, providing a handsome and organized holder for your guy's accoutrements. Stitch it up in denim with cotton-webbing trim and you've got a dapper looking kit that's both rugged and refined. Dads and grads can be hard to sew for, but this project will fit the bill for the guys on your list.

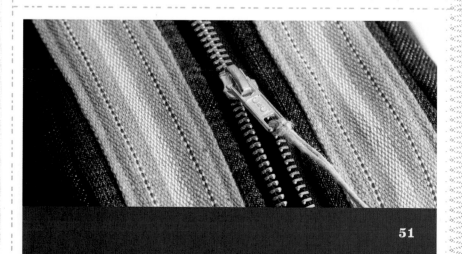

prepare materials

Using the patterns, cut from the main fabric, lining, interfacing, and fusible fleece:

2 Top Panels

2 Front/Back pieces

2 Side/Bottom Gusset pieces

2 Exterior Pockets

Using the pattern, cut from the lining and the interfacing:

2 Interior Pocket pieces

Using the pattern, also cut from the interfacing:

1 Interior Pocket piece

From the trim, cut:

2 lengths measuring 16" (40.5 cm) for the top panel trim

2 lengths measuring 3" (7.5 cm) for the grab tabs

1 length measuring 7" (18 cm) for the handle (or 2 lengths to double if the trim is lightweight)

Fuse the Interfacing

1 Stabilize the fabrics. Following the manufacturer's instructions, fuse the cut fleece pieces to the wrong side of their corresponding pieces cut from the main fabric.

2 Fuse the cut interfacing pieces to the wrong side of their corresponding pieces cut from the lining fabric. Transfer all pattern markings to the wrong (stabilized) sides of each cut piece with a disappearing-ink fabric marker.

Sew the Exterior Pockets

3 Layer one Exterior Pocket piece cut from the main fabric on top of one Exterior Pocket lining piece, right sides together. Sew across the top edge with a ¼" (6 mm) seam allowance. Open up the seam and press with the wrong sides together.

4 Change the thread in your sewing machine to heavy-duty denim thread, then topstitch the seam at ⅜" (1 cm).

5 Cut a 1½" (3.8 cm) length of the hook-and-loop tape. Pin one side of it ½" (1.3 cm) down from the top edge of the Exterior Pocket lining, centered on the pattern marking.

Topstitch ¹⁄₁₆" (2 mm) from the edge around the perimeter of the tape, then stitch an X in the center of the rectangle, backstitching at the beginning and end of your stitching.

6 Place the pocket on a Front/Back piece, right side up, with the sides and bottom edges aligned. Mark where the loop side of the hook-and-loop tape on the pocket touches and pin the corresponding piece onto the Front/Back. Set the pocket aside.

Switch back to your coordinating thread. Topstitch the hook-and-loop tape into place onto the Front/Back piece.

7 Place the pocket back on top of the Front/Back piece, right side up, and machine baste the sides and bottom edges together ⅛" (3 mm) from the edge.

8 Repeat Steps 3 through 7 to sew the second Exterior Pocket piece.

Trim the Top Panels and Install the Zipper

9 Align the 16" (40.5 cm) length of trim down the length of a Top Panel piece, right side up and centered side to side. Topstitch the length of the trim ¹⁄₁₆" (2 mm) from each of the edges.

Repeat for the second Top Panel piece with a second piece of trim.

10 Layer one Top Panel piece on one side of the zipper tape, right sides together, centering the zipper end to end on the panel **(figure 1)**. Pin, then sew with a ¼" (6 mm) seam allowance using a zipper foot.

Repeat with the other Top Panel and zipper tape.

Press seams to one side. Using the heavy-duty thread, topstitch the panel seams ⅛" (3 mm) from the edge.

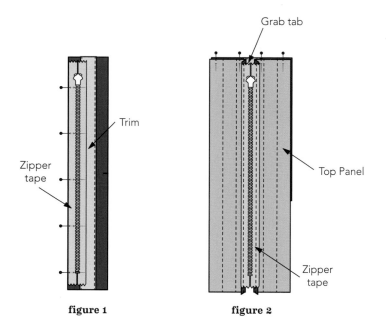

figure 1

figure 2

Grab tab

Trim

Zipper tape

Top Panel

Zipper tape

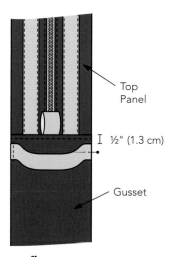

figure 3

Top Panel

½" (1.3 cm)

Gusset

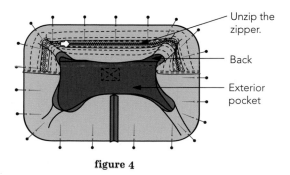

figure 4

Unzip the zipper.

Back

Exterior pocket

Sew the Gussets

11 Fold one grab tab length of trim in half, aligning the raw edges. Pin the raw edges of the tab to the top edge of a Side/Bottom Gusset piece, centering it with the loop hanging down. Using the coordinating thread, sew with a ⅛" (3 mm) seam allowance.

Repeat the process for the second grab tab and Side/Bottom Gusset piece.

12 Layer one Side/Bottom Gusset with the sewn zipper panels, right sides together. Align the end of the grab tab with one end of the sewn top panel **(figure 2)**.

Pin and sew across the ends with a ¼" (6 mm) seam allowance, sandwiching the grab tab between layers. Press the seam down and topstitch ⅛" (3 mm) away from the seam on the gusset side of the seam, using the heavy-duty denim thread again.

Repeat for the other end of the zipper panel, sewing the second grab tab between the Side/Bottom Gusset and the Top Panel ends.

13 Match the unsewn ends of the two Side/Bottom Gusset pieces, right sides together, and sew with a ¼" (6 mm) seam allowance. Then press the seams to one side.

Sew the Handle

14 If the trim you're using is a bit flimsy, you may want to edgestitch two layers of trim together to create a double layer handle that will be sturdier.

Pin each end of the case handle to the side edges of the gusset, ½" (1.3 cm) below the gusset seam near the zipper pull. Machine baste the handle at ⅛" (3 mm) **(figure 3)**.

Assemble the Exterior Case

15 Unzip the zipper, then pin the sewn top panel and gusset to the back of the case, matching the center points and the bottom gusset seam with the back.

The top panel and gusset seams should be placed about ½" (1.3 cm) below the top edge of the exterior pocket. Pin, then stitch the sewn panel to the back of the case with a ¼" (6 mm) seam allowance **(figure 4)**.

16 Trim the curved seam allowances with pinking shears to ³⁄₁₆" (5 mm). Press the bottom and top edge seams to one side. Be sure to use a press cloth when pressing the fusible fleece because it has a low melting temperature.

17 Repeat Steps 15 and 16, sewing the front of the case to the other edge of the sewn top panel and gusset.

Sew the Interior Pockets

18 Align the Interior Pocket pieces right sides together and pin. Sew the top and sides with a ¼" (6 mm) seam allowance. Turn right side out through the bottom opening and press.

19 Fold the top edge of the sewn interior pocket at the first marked line and press. Edgestitch down the fold about 1½" (3.8 cm) from the top edge, ⅛" (3 mm) from the fold **(figure 5)**.

Repeat at each of the other vertical pattern marks.

20 Now fold the pocket vertically at the pairs of markings to create pleats. Match the middle pleats in the center and press. Pin the pleats in place. The pocket should measure about 8" (20.5 cm) in width after pleating.

21 Layer the pocket, right side up, onto one Front/Back lining piece, aligning the bottom edges and centering the pocket side to side. Pin it into position and sew the sides and bottom edge with a ⅛" (3 mm) seam allowance.

22 Lift the center pleats and stitch vertically down the center of the pocket between the two pleats **(figure 6)**.

Assemble the Lining

23 Press a ¼" (6 mm) hem on one long side of each Top Panel lining piece. With the fold toward the center and spaced about ¾" (2 cm) apart, match and pin one set of panel ends to the end of one Side/Bottom Gusset lining piece, right sides together. Sew with a ¼" (6 mm) seam allowance and press.

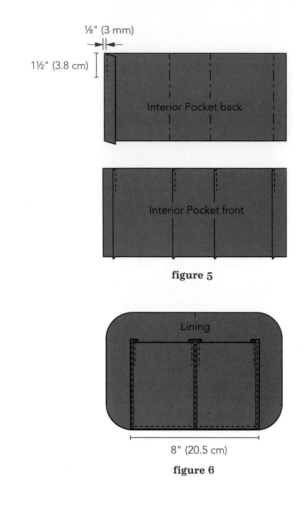

⅛" (3 mm)

1½" (3.8 cm)

Interior Pocket back

Interior Pocket front

figure 5

Lining

8" (20.5 cm)

figure 6

24 Repeat, sewing the other set of Top Panel lining ends to the other Side/Bottom Gusset lining piece. Sew the bottom lining gusset seam right sides together.

25 Pin the sewn lining panel to the edge of the back lining piece, right sides together, matching center points and the bottom gusset seam with the back lining piece.

Sew together with a ⅜" (1 cm) seam allowance. Repeat this step, sewing the front lining piece to the other edge of the sewn lining panel.

26 Trim the curved seam allowances with pinking shears. Press the straight seam allowances open.

Attach the Lining

27 With the exterior case and the case lining wrong sides out, match the bottom seams and pin the outer seam allowances together. With a needle and thread, whipstitch (see Techniques, page 154) the exterior and lining seam allowances together to the beginning of each curve. Turn the lining case right side out over the exterior case.

28 Align the exterior and lining seam allowances where the Top Panel pieces meet the front and back of the case. Whipstitch these seam allowances together in the same fashion.

Handstitch the folded edges of the Top Panel lining to the zipper tape.

stitched with meaning
Turn worn out camos into a smart case

Sew up the Gentleman's Travel Case in "business casual" fabrics by salvaging material from a cast-off pair of chinos or camouflage-style pants and an old dress shirt. The long narrow pattern pieces of the case are the right shape for cutting from the legs of a larger pair of pants. Dress shirts have a great expanse of fabric, so you'll have plenty to spare for another project, too.

new and **little**

Every time a new baby comes into the world, it means there is another person to sew for! This chapter has eight adorable projects to sew for babies, toddlers, and big kids. Tap into your inner child and get ready to play with bold colors, soft fabrics, and fun projects to make for the little ones in your life.

kinetic felt
{ baby mobile }

finished size
9" × 24" (23 × 61 cm)

what you'll need

9" × 3" (23 × 7.5 cm) piece of green 3 mm wool felt

9" × 2" (23 × 5 cm) pieces of red, blue, and orange 3 mm wool felt

9" × 1" (23 × 2.5 cm) piece of pink 3 mm wool felt

⅛ yd (11.5 cm) of blue wool-blend felt

Coordinating thread

2 blue felt balls, 1 cm in diameter

1 pink felt ball, 2 cm in diameter

8 red felt balls, 2 cm in diameter

5 yd (4.6 m) baker's twine

9" (23 cm) wooden embroidery hoop

Your sewing box

Rotary cutter, self-healing mat, and ruler

Aleene's Original Tacky Glue

Large needle

Eye-catching shape, color, and motion are what mobiles are all about. Felt is the perfect material for mobiles. It's light, it's easy to work with, and it holds its shape. Each motif in this mobile is made with narrow strips stitched with points and curves to create a bold, clean look. Suspended above a crib or high in a playroom, it's fun for little people and big ones alike.

The Kinetic Felt Baby Mobile is intended for decoration and is not a toy. Hang high within baby's sight but out of reach.

prepare materials

Using a rotary cutter, self-healing mat, and ruler, cut the 3 mm felt into ½" (1.3 cm) wide strips, cutting in the lengthwise direction.

From the orange strips, cut:

1 length measuring 9" (23 cm) for the fish

1 length measuring 1¾" (4.5 cm) for the fish

4 lengths measuring 2" (5 cm) for one diamond

From the blue strips, cut:

1 length measuring 7" (18 cm) for the bird

1 length measuring 2½" (6.5 cm) for the bird

1 length measuring 3½" (9 cm) for the bird

4 lengths measuring 2" (5 cm) for one diamond

From the red strips, cut:

4 lengths measuring 1" (2.5 cm) for the tulip

1 length measuring 4½" (11.5 cm) for the tulip

2 lengths measuring 3" (7.5 cm) for one heart

From the green strips, cut:

1 length measuring 7" (18 cm) for the bunny

2 lengths measuring 2½" (6.5 cm) for the bunny

2 lengths measuring 3½" (9 cm) for the tulip

1 length measuring 5½" (14 cm) for the hanger loop

From the pink strips, cut:

2 lengths measuring 3" (7.5 cm) for one heart

From the blue wool-blend felt, cut:

2 lengths measuring ½" (1.3 cm) wide and as long as possible. About 60" (152.5 cm) total is needed for wrapping the hoop.

A Note about Heavy Felt

When sewing two layers of 3 mm felt together, pin the layers by sticking a straight pin through the layers at a 45-degree angle. Don't try to bring the pin back up through the layers again—the felt is too thick.

When sewing a seam through two strips, begin in the center of the seam, backstitch to the beginning edge, sew through the width, and then backstitch to the center again. Starting this way will give the presser foot and feed dogs the necessary traction and will double-stitch the seam. Trim threads close.

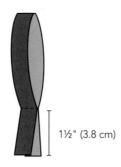

1½" (3.8 cm)

figure 1

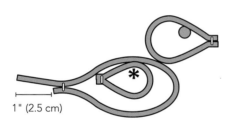

figure 2

1" (2.5 cm)

figure 3

figure 4

Make the Animals

1 Create the body of the fish by folding the 9" (23 cm) orange felt strip in half, aligning the cut ends. Pin and sew through both layers, 1½" (3.8 cm) from the cut ends (**figure 1**). This creates the division between the body and the tail.

2 Align the ends of a 1¾" (4.5 cm) long orange strip with the ends of the first strip. Pin and sew across the ends ⅛" (3 mm) from the edges, creating the end of the tail.

3 Cut two small triangle fins from orange felt scraps, estimating their size and shape. Apply a small line of craft glue to one edge of one triangle and press it into the top of the fish, centering it on the strip side to side. Repeat to create a lower fin with the second triangle.

4 Glue a small blue felt ball inside the fish's body loop near the front for the eye (**figure 2**). Allow the glue to dry.

5 Create the bird's body by folding the 7" (18 cm) blue felt strip with the ends offset by 1" (2.5 cm). Pin and sew together ⅛" (3 mm) from the end of the overlap.

6 For the wing, fold the 2½" (6.5 cm) blue felt strip in half, aligning the cut ends. Pin and sew through both layers ⅛" (3 mm) from the ends. Repeat for the head, using the 3½" (9 cm) blue felt strip.

7 Apply a dab of glue to one side of the wing and insert it inside the body. Press the wing to the underside of the top strip of the body.

8 Apply a dab of glue to one side of the bird's head and press it to the top strip of the body. Glue a small blue felt ball inside the head near the front for the eye (**figure 3**). Allow the glue to dry.

9 To make the bunny, measure and mark a line 3" (7.5 cm) from the end of the 7" (18 cm) long green felt strip. Create the head and body by applying glue to each cut end of the strip and pressing the glued ends into either side of the strip at the marking, making a figure-eight shape. Secure with a pin until dry.

10 For the ears, fold one 2½" (6.5 cm) green felt strip in half, aligning the cut ends. Pin and sew through both layers ⅛" (3 mm) from the ends. Repeat for the other ear. Apply glue to the ends of the ears and press them into the top of the head.

11 Apply a dab of glue to the pink felt ball and place it inside the body at the bottom for the bunny's tail (**figure 4**, page 61). Secure with a pin until dry.

Make the Tulip

12 To make the tulip, create a V shape by layering two 1" (2.5 cm) red felt strips, aligning the cut ends. Pin and sew through both layers ⅛" (3 mm) from one set of ends (**figure 5**). Repeat with two more 1" (2.5 cm) strips to create a second V.

13 Layer and sew one strip from each V shape to the other to create a W. These will become the points of the tulip. Align one end of the 4½" (11.5 cm) red felt strip with one end of the W. Pin and sew through both layers ⅛" (3 mm) from the edge. Bend the 4½" (11.5 cm) strip around to meet the other end of the W, then sew the ends ⅛" (3 mm) from the edge.

14 For the leaves, fold one 3½" (9 cm) green felt strip in half, aligning the cut ends. Pin and sew through both layers ⅛" (3 mm) from the ends. Repeat for the other leaf.

15 Apply a dab of glue to the sides of the leaves and press to the bottom curve of the tulip. Apply another dab of glue where the two leaves meet (**figure 6**).

Make the Shapes

16 Create the hearts by aligning the ends of two 3" (7.5 cm) red felt strips. Pin and sew through both layers ⅛" (3 mm) from the edge. Bend the strips away from each other to create the top curves of the heart. Align the unsewn ends, pin, and sew together ⅛" (3 mm) from the edge to create the bottom point of the heart.

17 Repeat with the two 3" (7.5 cm) pink felt strips to create the pink heart (**figure 7**).

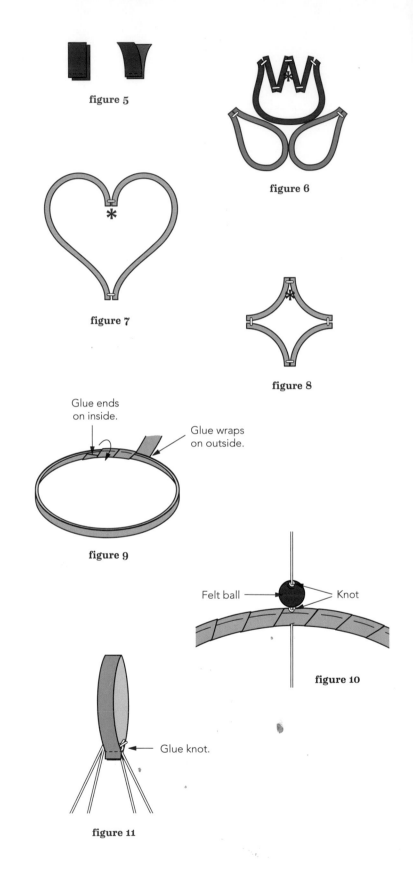

figure 5

figure 6

figure 7

figure 8

Glue ends on inside.

Glue wraps on outside.

figure 9

Felt ball — Knot

figure 10

Glue knot.

figure 11

18 For the orange diamonds, create the first V shape by layering two 2" (5 cm) orange felt strips, aligning the cut ends. Pin and sew through both layers ⅛" (3 mm) from one set of ends. Repeat with two more 2" (5 cm) orange felt strips to create the second V.

19 Align the unsewn ends of each V with each other and sew each ⅛" (3 mm) from the ends to create a diamond shape.

20 Repeat with the four 2" (5 cm) blue felt strips to create the blue diamond **(figure 8)**.

Wrap the Hoop

21 Loosen the screw on the outer embroidery hoop and remove the inner hoop (the outer hoop will not be used for this project).

Apply a small dab of glue on the inside of the inner hoop. Place the end of one of the wool-blend felt strips in the glue, angling the end 45 degrees. Apply a thin line of glue onto the outside of the hoop a few inches at a time. Wrap the felt strip around the hoop onto the glue, keeping the 45-degree angle and pushing each wrap right up next to the one before with no overlap **(figure 9)**.

When you use all of the first strip, glue the tail end to the inside of the hoop and then begin again, on the inside, gluing another strip.

Continue gluing and wrapping in this manner until the hoop is covered.

22 Using a disappearing-ink fabric marker, mark the top edge of the hoop in quarters at north, south, east, and west. Make a second set of marks in between each of those, for eight evenly spaced marks.

String the Shapes

23 Thread a large needle with a 26" (66 cm) length of baker's twine and knot the end. Following the asterisk (*) indications on the figures for each animal, insert the needle from the underside of the felt strip and out through the top of each animal.

24 Starting with the bird, stitch up through the inside of the hoop at the north mark, through the wrapped felt, emerging out the top of the hoop. Leave a 10" (25.5 cm) length of baker's twine between the bird and the hoop.

25 Take a small stitch in the felt at the top of the hoop and tie a knot in the twine. Then stitch through a 2 cm red felt ball. Tie a knot in the twine at the top of the felt ball **(figure 10)**. Do not trim the excess length; just let it hang down for now.

26 Follow Step 25 for the fish, bunny, and tulip at the south, east, and west marks.

27 Repeat Step 23 for the hearts and diamonds, starting with a 12" (30.5 cm) length of baker's twine. Following the asterisk (*) indications on the figures for each shape, insert the needle from the underside of the felt strip and out through the top of the shape.

28 Next, stitch up through the inside of the hoop on one of the in-between marks and through the wrapped felt, emerging out of the top of the hoop. Leave a 5" (12.5 cm) length of baker's twine between the shape and the hoop.

29 Take a small stitch in the felt at the top of the hoop, then stitch through a 2 cm red felt ball. Stitch back down through the ball, then knot off the twine at the base and trim the excess. Apply a small dab of glue on the knot under the felt ball.

30 Repeat this for both hearts and diamonds, alternating shapes at the in-between marks.

Make the Hanger Loop

31 To create the hanger loop, fold one 5½" (14 cm) green felt strip in half, aligning the cut ends. Pin and sew through both layers ⅛" (3 mm) from the ends.

32 Pick up two of the four baker's twine strands left from stringing the shapes and thread them through the loop. Thread the other two strands through the loop from the opposite direction. As evenly as possible, tie the strands together in a square knot.

33 Trim the excess and slide the knot down into the seamed point of the hanger loop. Apply a dab of glue on top of the knot and pinch the loop to secure the knot **(figure 11)**.

patchwork bears
{ baby quilt }

finished size
38" × 38" (96.5 × 96.5 cm)

what you'll need

Patchwork Bears Baby Quilt patterns on side D of the insert

3–4 yd (2.7–3.7 m) total of assorted quilting cottons or 13 assorted fat quarters plus ¼ yd (23 cm) each for the inner and outer borders

⅔ yd (61 cm) of muslin

1½ yd (1.4 m) of backing fabric

1½ yd (1.4 m) of batting

¼ yd (23 cm) of fusible webbing

Coordinating thread

Coordinating embroidery floss and needle (optional)

Your sewing box

Rotary cutter, self-healing mat, and ruler

Small, sharp scissors

Handsewing needle (optional)

Binding clips (optional)

Spray starch (optional)

New babies are one of the best excuses to sew something cute. Welcome a little one into the world with the Patchwork Bears Baby Quilt. This quilt, adorable either as a wall hanging or used for tummy time and snuggling, features four friendly bear faces with a seamed edge reverse appliqué. Combine bold fabrics for baby's visual stimulation or blend soft pastels and calm neutrals to lull baby off to dreamland.

prepare materials

For the quilt blocks, cut from the assorted fabrics:

4 squares measuring 12¼" × 12¼" (31 × 31 cm) for the window blocks

4 squares measuring 10" × 10" (25.5 × 25.5 cm) for the bear faces

5 squares measuring 11½" × 11½" (29 × 29 cm) for the plain blocks

Cut from the muslin:

4 squares measuring 12¼" × 12¼" (31 × 31 cm) for the window blocks

For the quilt borders, cut from the assorted fabrics:

2 strips measuring 1" × 33½" (2.5 × 85 cm) (or the width of your fabric) for the inner border

2 strips measuring 1" × 34½" (2.5 × 87.5 cm) (or the width of your fabric) for the inner border

2 strips measuring 2½" × 34½" (6.5 × 87.5 cm) (or the width of your fabric) for the outer border

2 strips measuring 2½" × 38½" (6.5 × 98 cm) (or the width of your fabric) for the outer border

For the quilt binding, cut from the assorted fabrics:

4 strips measuring 2¼" (5.5 cm) × the width of your fabric for the binding

Use a pencil to trace the appliqué patterns onto the fusible webbing, then loosely cut around the pencil lines:

8 Ear Appliqués

8 Eye Appliqués

4 Nose Appliqués

Fuse the Appliqués

1 Using an iron, fuse each appliqué piece of webbing to the wrong side of the assorted fabrics. Cut out each shape directly on the pencil line and peel off the paper backing.

Sew the Face Blocks

2 Using the Face Appliqué pattern, trace the outline onto the center of a muslin square with a disappearing-ink fabric marker. The top of the head should be about 3½" (9 cm) below the top of the square.

Repeat with the other three muslin squares.

3 Place each muslin square on top of a 12¼" × 12¼" (31 × 31 cm) quilting cotton square, with right sides facing up. Pin together around the traced face shape. Using a straight stitch, carefully machine stitch on top of the marked outline of the bear face on the muslin.

4 Use small, sharp scissors to cut through both layers of fabric inside the stitched face shape, leaving a ¼" (6 mm) seam allowance. Clip the curved seam allowances about every ¼" (6 mm) and trim off the seam allowance points at the base of the ears. This will create a window block **(figure 1)**.

5 Turn the block right side out by pulling the muslin square through the shaped hole to the wrong side of the quilting cotton square. Work out the curves with your fingers. Use a turning tool to work out the points at the base of the ears.

Press the block into shape with an iron. Take your time to smooth the curves to get a nice, crisp edge with no muslin showing from the right side of the block **(figure 2)**.

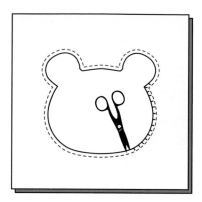

Clip seam allowances.

figure 1

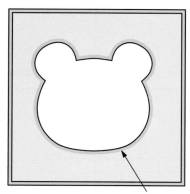

Seam allowances
are between layers.

figure 2

6 Place one 10" (25.5 cm) bear face square, right side up, behind each window block, right side up, and pin together. Carefully top-stitch around the face, ⅛" (3 mm) from the edge of the opening. Turn the block over and trim away the excess muslin and bear face square fabric, ¼" (6 mm) away from the stitch line.

7 Repeat this process for all four window blocks. Square up each one, trimming to 11½" × 11½" (29 × 29 cm).

8 Place two Ear Appliqués, two Eye Appliqués, and one Nose Appliqué, webbing side down, onto the right side of each bear face. Cover with a press cloth and fuse the shapes in place.

By machine or by hand with coordinating embroidery floss, blanket-stitch (see Techniques, page 154) the edge of each fused shape.

Sew the Quilt Top

9 Following the layout in **figure 3** (page 68), arrange the bear face blocks and plain blocks into three rows. Use a ¼" (6 mm) seam allowance to sew the blocks into rows, then sew the rows together, taking care to match the intersecting seams.

To help keep the seams matched so you'll get nice solid points, press each row in the opposite direction of the one below it. It should go like this: On the top row, press all seams to the left. On the middle row, press all seams to the right. On the bottom row, press all seams to the left. This will almost guarantee each joining seam will nest into the previous row.

10 Using a ¼" (6 mm) seam allowance, first sew the 1" × 33½" (2.5 × 85 cm) inner border strips to each side of the quilt top. Second, sew the 1" × 34½" (2.5 × 87.5 cm) inner border strips to the top and bottom of the top. Third, sew the 2½" × 34½" (6.5 × 87.5 cm) outer border strips to the sides of the quilt top. Last, sew the 2½" × 38½" (6.5 × 98 cm) outer border strips to the top and the bottom.

If you cut your border pieces to the width of your fabric, sew each to the top as described, then trim away the excess.

11 Press the quilt top and trim away the excess threads.

Quilt and Bind the Bear Blanket

12 Iron your quilt backing fabric smooth. Lay the quilt backing onto the floor, wrong side facing up. Layer the batting onto the quilt backing, smoothing out any wrinkles. Layer the quilt top, right side up, on top of the batting. Be sure to center the top so there are at least 2" (5 cm) of excess batting and backing on all sides.

13 Baste the quilt sandwich together starting from the center and working your way out. (See Techniques, page 154, for tips on basting a quilt.)

14 Quilt the sandwich by machine or by hand. Start quilting from the center and work your way out toward the edges.

The sample quilt shown is quilted in a free-motion squiggle pattern.

15 Trim the quilt to 38" (96.5 cm) square.

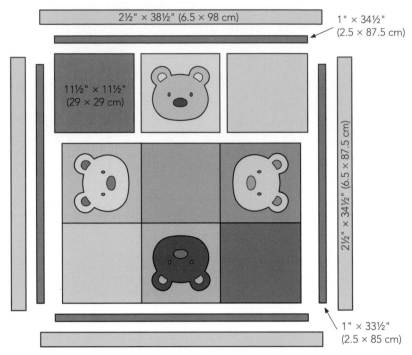

2½" × 38½" (6.5 × 98 cm)

1" × 34½" (2.5 × 87.5 cm)

11½" × 11½" (29 × 29 cm)

2½" × 34½" (6.5 × 87.5 cm)

1" × 33½" (2.5 × 85 cm)

figure 3

16 Sew the binding pieces together by placing together one end from two pieces, right sides together at a right angle. Sew at a 45-degree angle, from the top left corner to the bottom right corner, across the ends. Trim the excess ¼" (6 mm) from the seam. Press the seam allowances open.

Repeat this process to create one long binding strip from all four of the pieces.

17 Press the binding strip in half lengthwise, wrong sides together. Align the raw edge of the binding with the raw edges of the quilt top and pin. Sew the binding to the quilt sandwich, using a ¼" (6 mm) seam and leaving a 5" (12.5 cm) tail of binding at the start.

As you stitch to each corner, fold the binding on the diagonal to miter the corners. (Refer to Techniques, page 154, for details on binding a quilt.)

18 As you approach the starting tail of the binding, unfold the binding and sew the ends, right sides together. Finish sewing to the front of the quilt sandwich. Press the binding away from the front.

19 Fold the binding toward the backing and pin or secure with binding clips. Stitch in the ditch from the front, catching the binding on the back as you sew, or handstitch the binding to the back of your quilt.

stitched with meaning
incorporate favorite baby clothes into your quilt

Some of the sweetest baby items are outgrown before they're worn more than a few times. Make the Patchwork Bears Baby Quilt more heartfelt by repurposing those early baby clothes or other meaningful items, such as lightweight swaddling blankets and crib sheets, for the appliquéd bear faces.

tagalong { teddy }

finished size
13" (33 cm) from ears to feet

what you'll need

Tagalong Teddy patterns on side C of the insert

¼ yd (23 cm) of cotton terry or other soft-textured knit such as Minky or velour for the bear body

8" × 8" (20.5 × 20.5 cm) piece of printed cotton for ears, tummy, and foot pads

6" × 11" (15 × 28 cm) piece of wool-blend felt for vest

2" × 3" (5 × 7.5 cm) piece of wool-blend felt for muzzle

1" × 1" (2.5 × 2.5 cm) squares of red, black, and gray wool-blend felt for heart, eyes, and nose

8½" × 11" (21.5 × 28 cm) piece of double-sided fusible webbing

Coordinating thread

Coordinating embroidery floss and needle

Polyester stuffing

Your sewing box

Ballpoint needle for your sewing machine

Pinking shears

Handsewing needle

Walking foot for your sewing machine (optional)

Tagalong Teddy knows how to be a good friend. With big ears for listening, soft paws to hold on to, and a sweet smiling face, this bear is sure to be a favorite companion for any little one. Based on simple, ragdoll-style construction, Tagalong Teddy is a great beginner-level stuffed animal. The removable vest can be customized by adding embroidered details, making it even more special.

As always, young children should be supervised when playing with handmade toys.

prepare materials

Using the patterns, cut from the knit fabric:

2 Bear Heads

2 Ears

2 Body pieces

2 Arms

2 reversed Arms

2 Legs

2 reversed Legs

1 Tail

Using the pattern, cut from the printed cotton:

2 Ears

Using the pattern, cut from the felt:

1 Vest

Using the patterns, trace the appliqués onto the fusible webbing with a pencil, then cut loosely outside of the pencil line:

1 Tummy

2 Foot Pads

1 Nose

1 Heart

2 Eyes

1 Muzzle

Fuse the Appliqués

1 Using an iron, fuse each piece of webbing to the wrong side of the desired appliqué felt or fabric. Cut out each shape directly on the pencil line and peel off the paper backing.

Embellish the Bear's Face and Body

2 Place the Muzzle piece right side up onto the right side of one of the Bear Head pieces, following the pattern placement guide. Cover with a press cloth and fuse to the head. Using embroidery floss, embroider the edge using a blanket stitch (see Techniques, page 154, for embroidery stitch directions).

3 Fuse the Nose and Eye pieces in place and use a small whipstitch around the edges with matching thread or floss. Add a white highlight to each eye by making a small French knot (just two wraps of embroidery floss around the needle).

4 Using gray embroidery floss, stitch the mouth and snout with a backstitch.

5 Place the Tummy piece right side up onto the right side of one of the Bear Body pieces, following the pattern placement guide. Cover with a press cloth and fuse to the body.

Using embroidery floss, embroider the edge using a blanket stitch.

6 Fuse the felt Heart piece to the teddy bear's chest in the same way, then whipstitch the edges to secure.

Sew the Ears

7 Place one printed cotton Ear piece on top of one terry Ear piece, right sides together. Pin, then sew with a ¼" (6 mm) seam allowance around the curve, leaving the straight ends open. Turn through the opening and press.

Fold the sewn ear in half, top to bottom, and stitch a ⅛" (3 mm) tuck from the back through all of the layers **(figure 1)**.

Repeat for the bear's second ear.

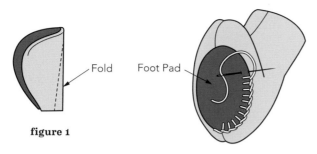

Fold

Foot Pad

figure 1

figure 2

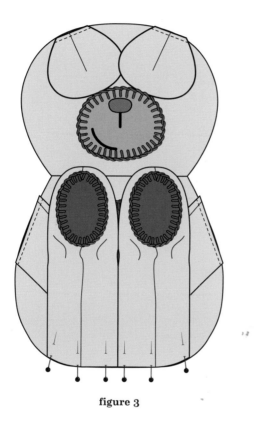

figure 3

Sew the Arms and Legs

8 Layer and pin two (one reversed) of the four Arm pieces right sides together. Sew with a ¼" (6 mm) seam allowance, leaving the short, straight end open.

Turn the arm right side out and fill with stuffing, leaving the last ½" (1.3 cm) unstuffed.

Repeat for the bear's second arm.

9 Layer and pin two (one reversed) of the four Leg pieces right sides together and sew with a ¼" (6 mm) seam allowance, leaving the short, straight end open.

Turn right side out and fill with stuffing, leaving the last ½" (1.3 cm) unstuffed.

10 Place one of the Foot Pad pieces onto the bottom of one of the feet, webbing side down. With an iron, carefully fuse it to the foot, covering the seam. Using embroidery floss, embroider the edge of the Foot Pad using a blanket stitch **(figure 2)**.

Repeat both steps for the bear's second leg.

Sew the Head to the Bear's Body

11 Layer the sewn ears, print side down, onto the right side of the embellished Head piece at the pattern markings, aligning the raw edges. Machine baste the ears to the head with a ⅛" (3 mm) seam allowance. Place the embellished Head piece right sides together onto the embellished Body piece, aligning the neck seam.

Pin and sew the Head to the Body with a ¼" (6 mm) seam allowance.

12 Repeat, sewing the neck seam for the back Head and back Body pieces.

A Note about Sewing Knits

Sometimes sewing knits can be tricky. It's important to use a ballpoint needle and plenty of pins to secure the layers of fabric and to sew slowly. If your machine has a walking foot normally used for quilting, using it to sew knits can help reduce stretching as you stitch.

Assemble the Bear

13 Following the pattern markings, layer the sewn and stuffed arms onto the front Body piece. Pin the raw edges of the arms along the sides of the Body. Machine baste ⅛" (3 mm) from the edge.

14 Layer the sewn and stuffed legs onto the front Body piece and pin the raw edges along the bottom of the Body. Machine baste ⅛" (3 mm) from the edge (**figure 3**, page 73).

15 Fold the arms in on top of the Body and let the legs hang down away from the Body. Layer the back head and body section on top of the front head and body section, right sides together. Pin, sandwiching the arms and ears between layers.

Sew around the perimeter, leaving the bottom edge open (**figure 4**). Trim the curved seam allowances with pinking shears, then turn the bear right side out.

16 Stuff the bear's head and body with stuffing. Ladder stitch (see Techniques, page 154) the bottom closed.

17 With a needle and thread, make a running stitch around the perimeter of the Tail piece. Partially gather the stitches and stuff the Tail. Pull tight and stitch it closed. Ladder stitch the sewn tail to the bear's behind.

18 To make the vest, fold the collar as indicated on the pattern with dashed lines. Stitch down the corners of the collar with an X of embroidery floss. Dress your bear!

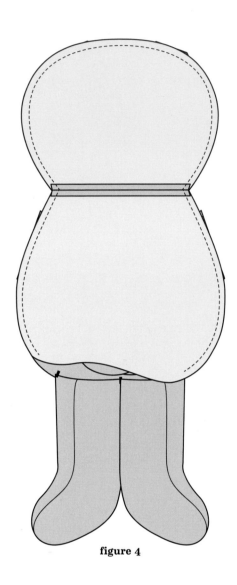

figure 4

stitched with meaning
turn outdated knits into cuddly teddy bears

For a super-lux stuffed bear, swap out the terry cloth for a buttery rich cashmere knit. Fine-gauge cashmere sweaters, especially those with outdated styling, can be found at thrift stores at an affordable price. Fuzzy fleece tops, velour leggings, and other soft knits are great opportunities for upcycling as well.

bib, rattle & burp
{ baby set }

finished size

Bib: 9½" × 11" (24 × 28 cm)

Wrist rattle: 3½" × 7" (9 × 18 cm)

Burp cloth: 9½" × 17½" (24 × 44.5 cm)

what you'll need

Bib, Rattle & Burp Baby Set patterns on side B of the insert

½ yd (45.5 cm) total of various cotton prints or solids

¾ yd (68.5 cm) of cotton terry

6" × 9" (15 × 23 cm) piece of fusible webbing

Felt scrap for the nose

Coordinating thread

Black and red embroidery floss and needle

4" (10 cm) strip of 1" (2.5 cm) wide hook-and-loop tape

1½" (3.8 cm) rattle insert

Your sewing box

Handsewing needle

Pinch of polyester stuffing

The Bib, Rattle & Burp Baby Set is a great bundle of stuff to give to a new bundle of joy. Parents will appreciate the adorable bunny bib for their wee drooler and a stack of pretty burp cloths ready to drape over a shoulder at a moment's notice. Babies will enjoy playful rattles that won't fall on the floor because they're strapped right to their chubby little wrists. If the baby is happy, everyone is happy!

As always, young children should be supervised when playing with handmade toys.

prepare materials

**Cut from various cotton prints
or solids:**

4 rectangles measuring 10" × 18" (25.5
× 45.5 cm) for the burp cloths

**Using the patterns, also cut from
various cotton prints or solids:**

1 Bib

1 Rattle Wristband

2 Rattle Ears

Cut from the terry cloth:

4 rectangles measuring 10" × 18" (25.5
× 45.5 cm) for the burp cloths

**Using the patterns, also cut from the
terry cloth:**

1 Bib

1 Rattle Head

2 Rattle Ears

**Using the appliqué patterns, trace
with a pencil onto the paper side of
the fusible webbing and cut loosely
around the pencil line:**

1 Bib Face

2 Inner Ears

2 Outer Ears

1 Bib Nose

1 Rattle Nose

Fuse the Appliqués

1 Using an iron, fuse each piece of webbing to the wrong side of the appliqué cottons and terry cloth. Cut out each shape directly on the pencil line and peel off the paper backing.

Sew the Bib

2 Layer each cotton print Inner Ear piece on top of each Outer Ear piece, right sides up. Place the layered ears and terry cloth Bib Face appliqué right side up onto the right side of the Bib piece, following the placement guide on the pattern. Make sure the face overlaps the ears.

3 Cover with a press cloth and fuse to the Bib. Using a narrow machine zigzag stitch, sew around the outer edge of the Bib Face and Outer Ears appliqués. Sew a zigzag or decorative blanket stitch around the edge of the Inner Ears appliqués.

4 Using embroidery floss, make two large French knots for the eyes and use a backstitch for the muzzle and whiskers. Fuse the nose in place and use a small whipstitch around the edges with matching thread or floss. (See Techniques, page 154.)

5 Layer the appliquéd Bib piece on top of the print Bib piece, right sides together, and pin around the perimeter. Sew with a ¼" (6 mm) seam allowance, leaving a 4" (10 cm) opening on one side for turning. Clip seam allowances on the inside curves and notch the outside curves.

Turn right side out through the opening and press, folding in the seam allowances at the opening. Topstitch the perimeter of the sewn bib ¼" (6 mm) from the edge, closing the side opening.

6 Following the placement on the pattern, sew the hook side of a 1" (2.5 cm) piece of hook-and-loop tape to the right side of one end of the bib by topstitching around the perimeter ⅛" (3 mm) from the edge. Repeat, sewing the loop side of the hook-and-loop tape to the wrong side of the other end of the bib.

Make the Wrist Rattle

7 Using embroidery floss, follow the placement indications on the patterns and embroider two French knots for the eyes and backstitch the muzzle. Fuse the felt Rattle Nose in place, then whipstitch the edges securely.

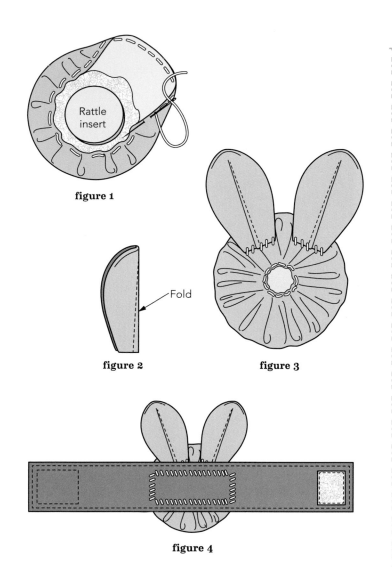

figure 1

Fold

figure 2   figure 3

figure 4

11 Fold the sewn ear in half top to bottom and stitch a ⅛" (3 mm) tuck from the back through all of the layers (**figure 2**).

Repeat both steps for the second ear.

Handstitch each ear to the back of the bunny head rattle with a whipstitch, overlapping the back of the rattle by ½" to ¾" (1.3 to 2 cm) (**figure 3**).

12 Fold the Rattle Wristband piece lengthwise and press to create a crease that runs the length of the rectangle. Open, then fold the raw edges in to meet the center crease and press. Open the folds and fold in each short end ¼" (6 mm) and press, taking care not to erase the previous creases. Refold the lengthwise folds so that the raw edges are all enclosed. Topstitch the edges of the wristband.

13 Sew the hook side of a 1" (2.5 cm) piece of hook-and-loop tape to one end of the wristband by topstitching around the perimeter ⅛" (3 mm) from the edge of the tape. Flip the wristband over and repeat, sewing the loop side of a 1½" (3.8 cm) piece of hook-and-loop tape to the opposite end of the wristband. This longer piece makes the wristband adjustable.

14 Handstitch the back side of the rattle to the center of the wristband, covering the gathers and the ends of the ears with the wristband. Whipstitch securely around the overlapping edges (**figure 4**).

Make the Burp Cloths

15 Layer one of the terry cloth rectangles and one of the print or solid cotton rectangles right sides together and pin. Sew together with a ¼" (6 mm) seam allowance, leaving a 3" (7.5 cm) opening on one side edge for turning. Clip off the seam allowance corners.

16 Turn the rectangles right side out through the opening. Press, folding in the seam allowances at the opening. Topstitch the perimeter of the burp cloth ³⁄₁₆" (5 mm) from the edge, closing the side opening as you sew.

17 Mark two lines across the width, sectioning the burp cloth into thirds—at about 6" (15 cm) and 12" (30.5 cm)—and topstitch.

18 Repeat with the other sets of rectangles to make three more burp cloths.

8 Double thread a handsewing needle and knot the end. From the wrong side of the Rattle Head piece, sew a running stitch ⅛" (3 mm) from the edge around the circle. Pull the thread to partially gather up the circle.

9 Place the rattle insert inside along with a pinch of polyester stuffing between the rattle and the circle (**figure 1**). Fully cinch up the circle, then stitch through the gathered edges on the back to secure.

10 Place one printed cotton Rattle Ear piece on top of one terry cloth Rattle Ear piece, right sides together. Sew with a ¼" (6 mm) seam allowance around the curve, leaving the straight ends open. Turn through the opening and press.

little flyer

{ cap }

finished size

Small (6M–12M): fits head circumference smaller than 19" (48.5 cm)

Medium (18M–24M): fits head circumference 19"–20" (48.5–51 cm) (shown)

Large (2T–4T): fits head circumference 20"–21" (51–53.5 cm)

what you'll need

Little Flyer Cap patterns on side C of the insert

½ yd (45.5 cm) of lightweight cotton main fabric

½ yd (45.5 cm) of lightweight cotton lining fabric

½ yd (45.5 cm) of lightweight woven fusible interfacing

½ yd (45.5 cm) of cotton batting

Coordinating thread

Two 2¼" (5.5 cm) lengths of ⅛" (3 mm) wide elastic

1 sew-through button, ½" (1.3 cm) in diameter

Your sewing box

Pinking shears

Tailor's ham or a rolled towel

Handsewing needle

All little nippers need a cool cap to keep their noggins warm. The Little Flyer Cap gives a child style and flexibility. It can be worn with flaps up on sunnier days or flaps down when a chilly breeze blows in. This design is baby friendly, foregoing long ties for small elastic loops on the flaps that secure on top with a button.

prepare materials

Using the patterns, cut from the main fabric, the lining, the interfacing, and the batting:

1 Center Crown Panel

2 Side Crown Panels

1 Brim

1 Ear Flap

1 reversed Ear Flap

A Note about Fit

For an accurate fit, choose the pattern size based on the circumference of the wearer's head. Measure the child's head with a tape measure placed just above the eyebrows.

Fuse the Interfacing

1 Fuse the interfacing pieces to the wrong sides of the main fabric pieces. Transfer all of the pattern markings to the fabric pieces with a disappearing-ink fabric marker.

Sew the Crown

2 Starting with the pieces cut from the main fabric, pin one of the Side Crown Panels to the Center Crown Panel with right sides together. Align the center points and distribute the fabric evenly around the curve of the crown **(figure 1)**.

If necessary, make ⅛" (3 mm) snips into the seam allowance of the Center Crown Panel to help ease the fabric into the Side Crown Panel.

3 Sew together using a ¼" (6 mm) seam allowance. Notch the curved seam allowances then press them open. Topstitch through the seam allowances ⅛" (3 mm) from both sides of the seam.

Repeat this step, sewing the second Side Crown Panel to the other side of the Center Crown Panel **(figure 2)**.

4 Layer the cut batting pieces onto the wrong side of the lining pieces for the Side Crown Panels and Center Crown Panel. Pin and sew the crown lining following the process in Step 2, except trim the seam allowances to ⅛" (3 mm) and omit the topstitching.

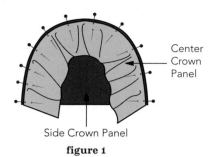

Center
Crown
Panel

Side Crown Panel

figure 1

figure 2

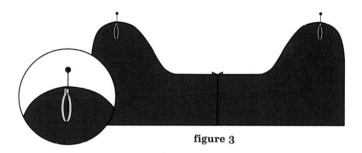

figure 3

figure 4

Make the Ear Flaps

5 Place the Ear Flap pieces cut from the main fabric right sides together. Stitch the short ends together with a ¼" (6 mm) seam allowance. Press the seam allowance open.

Repeat with the Ear Flap pieces cut from the lining fabric, layering the batting pieces onto the wrong side of the lining before you sew them.

6 Fold one length of elastic in half to create a small loop. Following the mark on the pattern piece, pin the ends to the right side of the ear flap **(figure 3)**. Repeat to create a loop on the right side of the second ear flap.

7 Place the sewn ear flaps—one made from the main fabric and one from the lining—with right sides together, sandwiching the elastic loops. Pin and sew around the perimeter with a ¼" (6 mm) seam allowance, leaving the long straight edge unstitched. With pinking shears, trim seam allowances to ⅛" (3 mm), turn flap right side out, and press.

8 Using a disappearing-ink fabric marker and ruler, mark the ear flaps with a 1" (2.5 cm) grid at a 45-degree angle. Topstitch along each line. Start at the seamed edge with a backstitch, then sew toward the open side of the flap **(figure 4)**.

Sew the Brim

9 Pin the Brim piece cut from lining to the Brim cut from the main fabric, right sides together. Sew around the outer curved perimeter with a ¼" (6 mm) seam allowance, leaving the inner, less-curved edge unstitched. With pinking shears, trim the seam allowances to ⅛" (3 mm), turn the brim right side out, and press.

10 Using a disappearing-ink fabric marker and ruler, mark the sewn brim with a 1" (2.5 cm) grid at a 45-degree angle. Topstitch along each line. Like the ear flaps, start at the seamed edge with a backstitch and sew toward the open side of the brim.

Assemble the Cap

11 Turn the crown sewn from the main fabric wrong side out. Place the ear flaps inside the crown, with the right sides of the main fabric together. Align the center back seam of the ear flaps with the center mark of the Center Crown Panel. Pin the raw edge of the ear flaps and the raw edge of the crown together.

12 Place the sewn brim inside the crown, with the right sides of the main fabric together. Align the center mark of the brim with the center mark of the Center Crown Panel and pin together along the raw edges of the crown. Then place the crown lining, right side out, inside the crown, sandwiching the brim and ear flaps **(figure 5)**.

The right side of the crown lining should be facing the lining sides of the brim and ear flaps. Repin around the entire perimeter, taking care to match all seams and pattern markings.

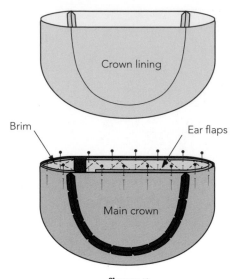

figure 5

Finish the Cap

13 Starting near the back of the crown, sew with a ¼" (6 mm) seam allowance around the perimeter of the crown through all layers. Leave a 3" (7.5 cm) opening at the back for turning. Trim the seam allowances to ⅛" (3 mm) to reduce bulk.

14 Turn the entire cap right side out through the 3" (7.5 cm) opening. Place the hat onto a tailor's ham or rolled towel and press. Use a ladder stitch (see Techniques, page 154) to handstitch the back opening closed.

15 Fold up the ear flaps and mark the top of the hat where the loops overlap, which should be the middle of the Center Crown Panel. Handsew a button securely through all layers at the mark. Pull the loops around the button to secure the ear flaps **(figure 6)**.

16 Fold the brim up. Hand-tack with a needle and thread in two spots where the brim meets the crown seams.

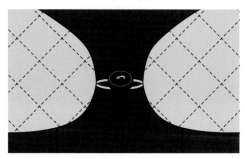

figure 6

stitched with meaning
remake an outgrown flannel shirt into a warm cap

Give the Little Flyer Cap a woodsman feel by upcycling a rustic flannel shirt for the exterior. Choose a plaid shirt that your child has outgrown or ask an uncle or grandpa to hand down an old favorite. A soft lightweight fleece for the lining will take this hat into the colder months with warmth and style.

hexie *the* turtle
{ floor pillow }

finished size

28" × 25" (71 × 63.5 cm), including the head, tail, and legs

what you'll need

Hexie the Turtle Floor Pillow patterns on side C of the insert

1¼ yd (1.1 m) total of a mix of 45" (114.5 cm) wide lightweight fabrics A for the turtle shell, pocket, and pillow back

¼ yd (23 cm) of 45" (114.5 cm) wide fabric B for the shell

1 yd (91.5 cm) of 45" (114.5 cm) wide fabric C for the head, legs, and tail

½ yd (45.5 cm) of 45" (114.5 cm) wide fabric D for the turtle shell and pocket lining

1 yd (91.5 cm) of woven-cotton fusible interfacing

⅔ yd (61 cm) of 45" (114.5 cm) wide cotton muslin

1 yd (91.5 cm) of cotton batting

Coordinating thread

2 black buttons, ½" (1.3 cm) in diameter, for the eyes

1 decorative button for the shell

1 bag of polyester stuffing

Your sewing box

Handsewing needle

Pinking shears

Quilting safety pins (optional)

At home in a child's bedroom or as a sleepover companion, Hexie the Turtle Floor Pillow is a playful friend to have around. The mixed-print patchwork shell can be made to coordinate with your child's room décor and would be fitting for a boy or girl depending on your fabric choices. Hexie even stashes special stuff (or a pair of jammies!) in a big pocket on the flip side.

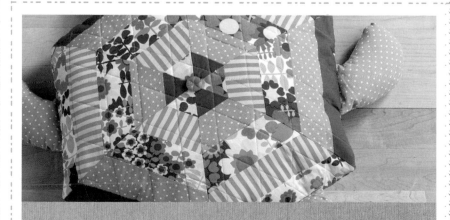

prepare materials

Cut from the mix of fabric A:

2 strips measuring 2½" × 44" (6.5 × 112 cm) for the shell

1 pillow back*

1 pocket front*

Cut from fabric B:

1 strip measuring 2½" × 44" (6.5 × 112 cm) for the shell

Cut from fabric C:

1 strip measuring 2½" × 44" (6.5 × 112 cm) for the shell

Using the patterns, cut from fabric C:

4 Legs

4 reversed Legs

1 Head Base

1 Head Top

1 reversed Head Top

1 Tail

1 reversed Tail

Cut from fabric D:

1 strip measuring 2½" × 44" (6.5 × 112 cm) for the shell

1 pocket lining*

Cut from the interfacing:

1 pillow back*

Cut from the batting:

1 pillow front*

1 pocket front*

Cut from the muslin:

1 pillow front*

*These will be cut later during the assembly process using sewn sections as patterns.

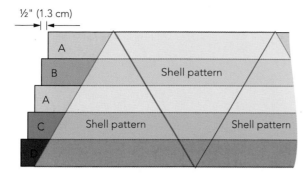

½" (1.3 cm)

A
B
A
C
D

Shell pattern

Shell pattern

Shell pattern

figure 1

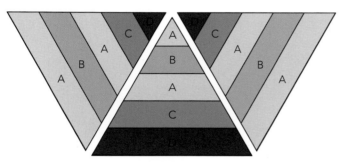

D
C
A
B
A
C
A
B
A

D
A
B
A
C
D
C
A
B
A

figure 2

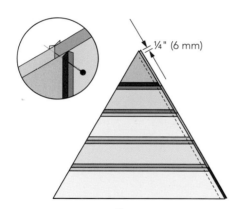

¼" (6 mm)

figure 3

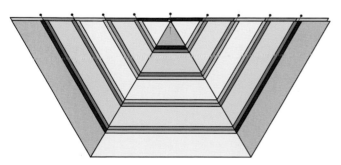

figure 4

Create the Pillow Top

Unless otherwise noted, sew all seams with a ¼" (6 mm) seam allowance.

1 Layer one fabric A strip on top of the fabric B strip, right sides together, offsetting the ends by ½" (1.3 cm). Pin and sew them together lengthwise. Press the seam allowance open.

2 Layer the second strip cut from fabric A on top of strip B, right sides together, aligning the long unsewn edge and offsetting the ends by another ½" (1.3 cm). Sew them together lengthwise. Press the seam allowance open.

Repeat, sewing the strips cut from fabric C to fabric A and from fabric D to fabric C (**figure 1**).

3 Using the Shell pattern and a disappearing-ink fabric marker, mark the sewn strips as shown in **figure 1**. Cut the strips into six triangles.

4 Arrange three of the triangular shell pieces on your work surface, right side up, alternating the order of the fabrics (**figure 2**).

Flip one triangle on top of a second triangle, right sides together. Pin one set of edges, taking care to align all seams. Place one pin directly through each seam. Sew along the edges, starting ¼" (6 mm) from the beginning of the triangle points (**figure 3**). Press the seam allowances open and repeat with the third triangle, starting ¼" (6 mm) away from the triangle point.

Repeat to create another set of three sewn triangles.

5 Layer both sets, right sides together, taking care to align and pin all seams precisely. Sew together, joining the two sets of triangles (**figure 4**). Press the seam allowances open.

With the wrong side facing up, trim the seam allowance points at the seam intersections to reduce bulk, especially at the center of the turtle shell pillow top.

6 Place the pillow top on your work surface, right side up. Using it as a template, cut one piece each from the batting, muslin, fabric A, and interfacing.

Set the fabric A and interfacing pieces aside to create the back of the pillow later.

Sandwich the batting between the wrong side of the pillow top and the muslin. Baste with quilting safety pins or hand-baste with a needle and thread to keep the layers from shifting. Stitch through all layers, quilting as desired.

The sample shown on page 88 is quilted in two directions at a 60-degree angle, 2" (5 cm) apart, to create a diamond pattern.

Create the Turtle Head, Tail, and Legs

7 Pin two Head Top pieces right sides together and sew the top seam. Align the sewn head top with the Head Base piece, right sides together. Pin the curved edges and sew, leaving the straight edges unsewn. Trim the seam allowances with pinking shears to ⅛" (3 mm).

Turn the head right side out and press the seams. Fill with polyester stuffing, leaving the last ½" (1.3 cm) near the opening unstuffed.

8 Place the two Tail pieces right sides together. Pin the curved edges and sew, leaving the straight edges unsewn. Trim the seam allowances with pinking shears to ⅛" (3 mm).

Turn the tail right side out and press seams. Fill with polyester stuffing, leaving the last ½" (1.3 cm) near the opening unstuffed.

9 Place one Leg piece and one reversed Leg piece right sides together. Pin the curved edges and sew, leaving the straight edges unsewn. Trim seam allowances with pinking shears to ⅛" (3 mm). Turn the leg right side out and press seams. Fill with polyester stuffing, leaving the last ½" (1.3 cm) near the opening unstuffed.

Repeat this step to make the other three legs.

10 Center and pin each stuffed turtle part to the corresponding straight edge of the shell pillow top, aligning the raw edges. Machine baste each piece by sewing ⅛" (3 mm) from the edge (**figure 5**).

Sew the Pillow Back and Pocket

11 Return to the pieces of interfacing and fabric A you cut in the shape of the pillow top. Fuse the interfacing to the wrong side of fabric A, creating the pillow back.

12 Using the pillow back as a pattern, cut the pocket front from fabric A, the

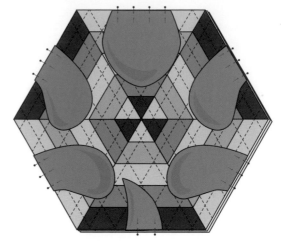

figure 5

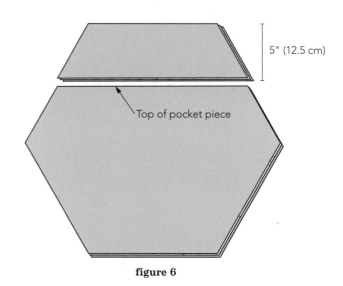

5" (12.5 cm)

Top of pocket piece

figure 6

pocket lining from fabric D, and a piece of batting. Then cut 5" (12.5 cm) of length off of all three pieces (**figure 6**).

13 Layer the pocket front on top of the batting, wrong side facing the batting, and pin. Quilt as desired.

14 Layer and pin the pocket lining onto the pocket front, right sides together, and sew across the top edge. Press the seam open and flip the lining to the wrong side. Topstitch the top of the pocket ¼" (6 mm) from the edge.

15 Place the pocket, lining side down, on top of the right side of the pillow back. Align the sides and bottom edges and pin. Machine baste the layers ⅛" (3 mm) from the edge.

Assemble the Pillow

16 Layer the sewn pillow back, right sides together, on the pillow top so that the top edge of the pocket is closest to the turtle's head. Pin all sides together, except the side with the tail, sandwiching the head and legs.

Carefully sew together using a ½" (1.3 cm) seam allowance, leaving the side with the tail unsewn. Trim the seam allowances to ¼" (6 mm) and clip the seam allowances at each corner. Turn the pillow right side out, press, and fill with polyester stuffing.

17 With a needle and thread, ladder stitch (see Techniques, page 154) the bottom opening closed. Sew two buttons on the head for eyes and one button in the center of the pillow top to decorate the shell.

stitched with meaning
transform sheets and shirts into comfortable pillows

Repurpose a mix of splashy vintage sheets to give Hexie a fun retro look that girls from toddler to tween will love. Just as cute for boys, upcycle a few men's oxford, chambray, and pinstripe shirts for a preppy pillow pal.

tiny *the* turtle
{ tooth fairy pillow }

Tiny the Turtle is a mini version of Hexie. Tiny's job is to keep small secrets—and other special things—safe in a hidden underbelly pocket. Tiny helps out the Tooth Fairy, too!

finished size

12" × 11" (30.5 × 28 cm) including the head, tail, and legs

what you'll need

Tiny the Turtle Tooth Fairy Pillow patterns on side C of the insert

¼ yd (23 cm) total of various prints or solid quilting cottons for the turtle shell

¼ yd (23 cm) of 45" (114.5 cm) wide fabric A for the pillow back and pocket

¼ yd (23 cm) of 45" (114.5 cm) wide fabric B for the head, legs, and tail

⅛ yd (11.5 cm) of 45" (114.5 cm) wide fabric C for the pocket lining

Small amount of polyester stuffing

2 black buttons, ¼" (6 mm) in diameter, for the eyes

1 decorative button for the shell

Your sewing box

Handsewing needle

prepare materials

Using the patterns, cut from the various prints and solids:

6 Shell triangles

From fabric A cut:

1 pillow back*

1 pocket front*

Using the patterns, cut from fabric B:

4 Legs

4 reversed Legs

1 Head Base

1 Head Top

1 reversed Head Top

1 Tail

1 reversed Tail

From fabric C cut:

1 pocket lining*

*These will be cut later during the assembly process using sewn sections as patterns.

Create the Pillow Top

1 Arrange three of the shell triangles on your work surface, right sides up, alternating the order of the assorted fabrics. Flip one triangle on top of a second triangle, right sides together. Sew together starting ¼" (6 mm) from the beginning of the triangle points (as in **figure 3** on page 89). Press the seam allowances open. Repeat with the third triangle.

Repeat to create another set of three triangles.

2 Layer the sets of triangles right sides together, taking care to pin the points precisely (as in **figure 4** on page 89). Sew together. Press the seam allowances open. With the wrong side facing up, trim the seam allowance points at the seam intersections to reduce bulk.

Create the Pillow Back and Pocket

3 Place the sewn turtle shell on your work surface, right side up. Use it as a pattern and cut a piece of fabric A to create the pillow back.

4 Using the pillow back as a pattern, cut the pocket front from fabric A and the pocket lining from fabric C. Cut off 1½" (3.8 cm) of length from the top of each of the three pieces (as in **figure 6** on page 90).

5 Layer the pocket lining onto the pocket front, right sides together, and sew across the top edge with a ¼" (6 mm) seam allowance. Press the seam open and flip the lining to the wrong side. Topstitch the top of the pocket ⅛" (3 mm) from the edge.

6 Place the pocket, lining side down, on top of the right side of the pillow back. Align and pin the sides and the bottom edges. Machine baste the layers ⅛" (3 mm) from the edge.

Finish Tiny the Turtle

7 To create the turtle's head, tail, and legs, follow Steps 7 through 10 for Hexie the Turtle Floor Pillow on page 90. Then assemble the Tiny the Turtle pillow by following Steps 16 and 17 of the instructions for Hexie on page 91.

finished size

Puppets: 3" × 1½"
(7.5 × 3.8 cm)

Stump: 6" × 4" (15 × 10 cm)

what you'll need

Forest Friends Finger Puppets patterns on side A of the insert

5" × 6" (12.5 × 15 cm) pieces of orange, black, and light gray wool-blend felt

6" × 6" (15 × 15 cm) square of white wool-blend felt

3" × 4" (7.5 × 10 cm) pieces of charcoal and dark green wool-blend felt

4" × 5" (10 × 12.5 cm) piece of rust wool-blend felt

2" × 3" (5 × 7.5 cm) piece of gold wool-blend felt

2" × 2" (5 × 5 cm) square of pink wool-blend felt

12" × 12" (30.5 × 30.5 cm) square of brown wool-blend felt

5" × 5" (12.5 × 12.5 cm) square of tan wool-blend felt

1½" × 2½" (3.8 × 6.5 cm) piece of light green wool-blend felt

Coordinating thread

Embroidery floss in orange, gray, white, black, and brown

Your sewing box

Aleene's Original Tacky Glue

Handsewing needle

Pinking shears

Freezer paper

Stiffen Quik fabric stiffening spray

Tissue paper

forest friends
{ **finger puppets** }

Kids big and small will be enamored with these felty forest creatures. Five different woodland finger puppets spark creative play, then tuck into their own hollow tree stump for handy storage. Felt scraps, a little sewing, a bit of glue, and a few embroidery stitches will bring these characters—and your kid's imagination—to life.

Because of the small components of this project, it is not suitable for children under three years of age. Young children should always be supervised when they are playing with handmade toys.

prepare materials

Trace all of the animal and stump patterns onto the matte side of the freezer paper. Loosely cut out the patterns around the lines (not on the lines). With a warm iron, gently press each of the freezer paper tracings, shiny side down, onto the associated color of felt, lightly fusing the patterns.

Cut out each shape on the solid line with scissors and on the dotted lines with pinking shears. Peel away the freezer paper.

Some patterns need to be used to cut out more than one felt piece. To reuse the freezer paper patterns, simply reposition, fuse, and cut.

From the orange felt, cut:

2 Body pieces for the fox

1 Fox Head

2 Fox Ears

1 Fox Tail

1 Owl Beak

From the white felt, cut:

2 Body pieces for the bunny

1 Bunny Head

2 Bunny Ears

1 Bunny Tail

3 Belly pieces for the fox, raccoon, and skunk

2 Owl Eyes

2 Fox Side Face pieces

1 Fox Tail Tip

1 Skunk Tail Stripe

1 Skunk Head Stripe

From the black felt, cut:

2 Body pieces for the skunk

1 Raccoon Mask

1 set of Raccoon Tail Stripes

2 Raccoon Inner Ears

1 Raccoon Nose

2 Fox Inner Ears

1 Fox Nose

From the charcoal felt, cut:

1 Skunk Head

1 Skunk Tail

From the light gray felt, cut:

2 Body pieces for the raccoon

1 Belly piece for the bunny

1 Raccoon Head

1 Raccoon Tail

2 Raccoon Ears

From the rust felt, cut:

2 Body pieces for the owl

1 Owl Ears piece

From the gold felt, cut:

1 Owl Tuft

1 Owl Belly

From the pink felt, cut:

2 Bunny Inside Ears

1 Skunk Nose

From the brown felt, cut:

1 Owl Wing

1 reversed Owl Wing

1 Stump Base

From the tan felt, cut:

1 Stump Top

5 Stump Sides

From the dark green felt, cut:

1 Big Leaf

2 Small Leaf pieces

From the light green felt, cut:

1 Inchworm

Assemble the Puppets and Add the Details

1 Place two Body pieces for one puppet together and pin. Sew around the perimeter ⅛" (3 mm) from the edge, backstitching at the beginning and end of the seam. Leave the bottom end open. Turn the body right side out.

2 Following the photo for placement, layer the components for each animal on top of the sewn body.

Lightly apply a small amount of craft glue to the back of each piece and press into place. Be sure to sandwich the puppet's Ear pieces (if any) between the Head and the Body pieces. Glue the Tail piece onto the back of the Body piece last.

3 Once the glue is dry, add some hand-stitched details. With a needle and three strands of embroidery floss, sew a running stitch around each Belly piece. Tie a French knot for each eye. Add one running stitch below the bunny's nose. (See Techniques for embroidery stitch instructions on page 154.)

Assemble the Stump

4 Start with two Stump Side pieces. Align the long sides, butting the cut edges together. Sew the butted pieces together using a wide zigzag stitch that straddles both pieces. If hand-stitching, whipstitch the butted edges together using a handsewing needle and thread (see **figure 1** for a diagram of butt seaming and turn to Techniques, page 154, for more information).

5 Sew a third Stump Side piece to the first pair, following the same process. Continue until all five Stump Sides are sewn together.

Bring the unsewn edge of the fifth side around to meet the unsewn edge of the first side. Butt together and zigzag. This is more easily done starting from the point shown in **figure 2**.

6 Align the edges and points of the sewn sides with the Stump Base piece and pin. Straight stitch them together around the perimeter ³/₁₆" (5 mm) from the edge. Carefully trim the seam allowance with pinking shears for a decorative effect **(figures 3a and 3b)**.

Create the Stump Top

7 Using a disappearing-ink fabric marker, transfer the spiral design from the template to the Stump Top piece. Stitch the spiral with a running stitch using three strands of brown embroidery floss.

8 Spray the Stiffen Quik onto the inside and outside of the stump and on both sides of the top in a light, even layer. Stuff the stump with tissue paper to hold the shape while it dries. Microwave or air dry the tree stump per the manufacturer's instructions.

9 Apply a thin stripe of craft glue, about ⅛" (3 mm) wide, along one edge of the Inchworm piece. Fold the edge of the felt over ¼" (6 mm) into the glue. Repeat, gluing and folding until the rectangle is in a tight skinny roll **(figures 4a, 4b, and 4c)**.

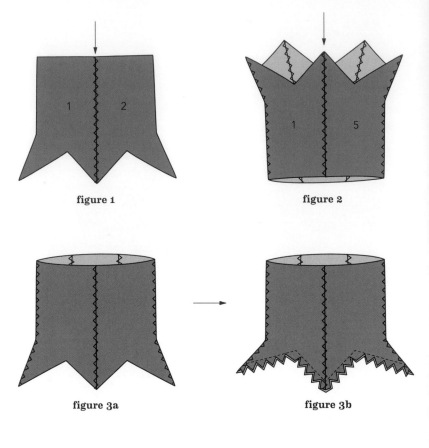

figure 1

figure 2

figure 3a

figure 3b

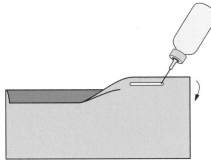

figure 4a

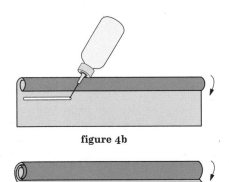

figure 4b

figure 4c

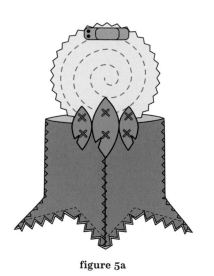

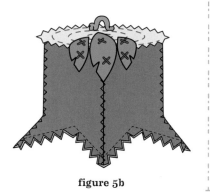

figure 5a   **figure 5b**

10 Once the roll is dry, stitch two black French knots onto one end for eyes. Fold the end with the eyes ¼" (6 mm) back on itself (with the eyes on top) and glue, securing it with a straight pin until dry.

Bend the inchworm into position and glue the head and tail near the edge of the stump top, securing with pins until dry.

11 Place one Big Leaf piece and two Small Leaf pieces at the back of the stump top and lightly glue into position as the hinges. With brown embroidery floss, stitch an X through each leaf at the lid and stump to secure to the stump **(figures 5a and 5b)**.

cuddly critter
{ mittens }

finished size

Small: fits hands 4½"–5¼" (11.5–13.5 cm) long

Medium: fits hands 5½"–6" (14–15 cm) long

Large: fits hands 6¼"–6¾" (16–17 cm) long

what you'll need

Cuddly Critter Mittens patterns on side B of the insert

⅓ yd (30.5 cm) of fleece in the main color: light gray for the raccoons or tan for the hedgehogs

⅓ yd (30.5 cm) of fleece in the accent color: dark gray for the raccoons or brown for the hedgehogs

Felt scraps: dark gray, light gray, and white for the raccoons or cream, brown, and white for the hedgehogs

Coordinating thread

Embroidery floss: gray and black for the raccoons or white and brown for the hedgehogs

⅜" (1 cm) buttons: 4 for the raccoon eyes or 2 for the hedgehog noses

Your sewing box

Freezer paper

Pinking shears

Aleene's Original Tacky Glue

Handsewing needle

Kids will be smitten with these adorable raccoon and hedgehog mittens. Designed with both a thumb and a pinky, these cuties are part mitten, part puppet. They're easy to put on (no right or left!) and make staying warm fun. Sew them up in soft cozy fleece with appliquéd felt details. They're easy to customize into whatever critter your little rug rat desires.

Because of the button eyes and nose, these mittens are not suitable for children under three years of age.

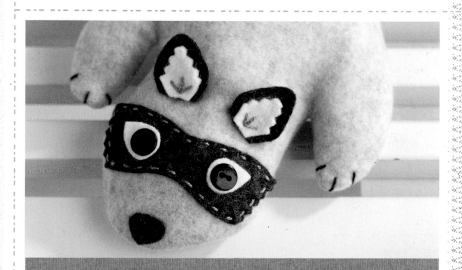

prepare materials

Using the desired size pattern, cut from the main fleece:

4 Hand pieces

From the accent fleece, cut two rectangles for the cuff:

Small: 2 rectangles measuring 6¼" × 3½" (16 × 9 cm)

Medium: 2 rectangles measuring 6½" × 4" (16.5 × 10 cm)

Large: 2 rectangles measuring 6¾" × 4" (17 × 10 cm)

To make the hedgehog, also cut from the accent fleece color:

Small: 6 rectangles measuring 1½" × 4" (3.8 × 10 cm)

Medium: 8 rectangles measuring 1½" × 4" (3.8 × 10 cm)

Large: 8 rectangles measuring 1½" × 4" (3.8 × 10 cm)

figure 1

Cut out the Critter Details

1 Trace the patterns for the face and body of the critter of your choice onto the matte side of freezer paper. Lightly iron the paper, shiny side down, onto the desired color of felt or fleece. Cut out the pieces on the traced lines, then peel off the freezer paper. Use pinking shears to cut on the dashed lines.

If you're making the small size raccoon mittens, trim ⅛" (3 mm) off the length of the Raccoon Mask piece on each end.

Sew the Mittens

2 Place one pair of Hand pieces right sides together and pin. Sew with a ¼" (6 mm) seam allowance around the perimeter, leaving the bottom straight edge open. Trim the seam allowance to ⅛" (3 mm) and clip the inner curves. Turn the mitten right side out.

3 Fold one cuff rectangle to match the short ends, right sides together. Sew the short ends together with a ¼" (6 mm) seam allowance. Trim the seam allowance to ⅛" (3 mm).

Fold the cuff over, wrong sides together, matching raw edges and aligning the seam with itself.

4 Slide the cuff over the wrist of the mitten, right sides together, aligning the raw edges and the cuff seam with one of the mitten seams. Pin the cuff to the mitten, distributing the fabric evenly **(figure 1)**.

Sew together, stitching from the inside of the mitten, with a ¼" (6 mm) seam allowance. Trim the seam allowance to ⅛" (3 mm) and turn back the cuff.

5 Repeat Steps 2 through 4 to sew the second Cuddly Critter Mitten.

6 If you're making the raccoon mittens, proceed with Steps 7 through 14. If you're making the hedgehog mittens, skip to Step 15.

Add the Raccoon Details

7 If you're making the raccoon mittens, first place one Raccoon Mask piece onto the top of one mitten across the main finger area. Tack in place lightly with a few dots of glue. Embroider a running stitch (see Techniques, page 154, for embroidery stitch instructions) around the perimeter of the mask in gray floss.

8 Place the eye patches on top of the mask and glue to secure. Place the button eyes on top of the patches. Sew the buttons down tightly, stitching through all of the layers.

9 Glue the Raccoon Nose piece onto the end of the mitten, then whipstitch around the edges to secure.

10 Layer one Raccoon Inner Ear piece onto one Raccoon Ear piece. Embroider three stitches into a V shape with gray floss (see photo). Repeat to make the second ear.

Glue the ears onto the mitten, then whipstitch the lower edge to secure.

11 With black floss, stitch three claws on the end of each paw (the pinky and the thumb). Glue, then whipstitch a Paw Pad piece onto the underside of each paw.

12 Tack the Tummy piece down with a few glue dots onto the underside of the mitten. Use a running stitch to embroider around the edge with gray floss.

13 Glue a set of Raccoon Tail Stripes onto the top of a Raccoon Tail piece. Layer the tail onto the back of the mitten, overlapping the cuff. Pin, then whipstitch around the perimeter with gray thread.

14 Repeat Steps 7 through 13 to complete the second raccoon mitten.

Add the Hedgehog Details

15 If you're making the hedgehog mittens, glue the felt Hedgehog Eyes onto the face about 1" (2.5 cm) apart and about 1" (2.5 cm) from the end of one mitten. Tack each one down with a white French knot highlight or whipstitch the edges to secure.

16 Sew the button nose to the center tip of the mitten.

17 Snip the 1½" × 4" (3.8 × 10 cm) rectangles into ⅜" (1 cm) fringe, stopping ¼" (6 mm) from the edge **(figure 2)**.

Place three fringed rectangles for the small size or four fringed rectangles for the medium or large size across the width of the mitten. Gently curve and slightly overlap the fringe front to back **(figure 3)**. Tack the straight edges with glue, then embroider with a running stitch along the straight edge.

18 Make two snips into the top of the Hedgehog Widow's Peak piece and center it above the eyes, overlapping the front row of fringe. Tack with glue, then whipstitch into place.

19 Referring to the photo, use a needle and thread to take a small tuck in the bottom of one Hedgehog Ear. Whipstitch the bottom edge to the mitten, placing it above the eyes and even with the widow's peak.

With brown floss, embroider two stitches into a V shape in the center of the ear.

Repeat to make the second ear.

20 With brown floss, stitch three claws on the end of each paw (the pinky and the thumb). Glue, then whipstitch a Paw Pad piece onto the underside of each paw.

21 Tack the Tummy piece down with a few dots of glue onto the underside of the mitten. Use a running stitch to embroider around the edge of the Tummy with brown floss.

22 Repeat Steps 15 through 21 to complete the second hedgehog mitten.

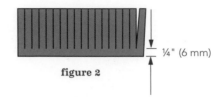

¼" (6 mm)

figure 2

figure 3

stitched with meaning
upcycle a favorite old baby blankie into new favorite mittens

An outgrown fleece jacket or stroller blanket would provide suitable material for a cozy pair of Cuddly Critter Mittens. High-tech poly fleece fabrics are often pill resistant and can look like new even after many uses. Turn a hand-me-down into handy mittens!

{ chapter three }

happy home

A *person's home* is where her heart is. It is her retreat from the world. Sewing gifts to celebrate someone's new house or to welcome a neighbor is a wonderful way to express your happiness for your friends. From hostess gifts to housewarming presents, you'll find nine cozy projects in this chapter to sew and give.

make & bake
{ apron }

When I say that I like to make things, I'm not talking about dinner! Most of my making happens at the sewing machine, not at the stove. So when it comes to spending time in the kitchen, putting on a little handmade apron sweetens the task. The Make & Bake Apron uses mostly straight-line stitching and sews together in a jiffy. The full apron style protects clothing from food splatters while the inverted pleat detailing keeps it cute. The Make & Bake Apron is a thoughtful gift for folks who love to cook, bake, or just look like they do.

prepare materials

Cut from the main fabric:

2 skirt pieces measuring 16" × 20"
(40.5 × 51 cm)

Using the pattern, also cut from the main fabric:

1 Apron Bib

1 reversed Apron Bib

Cut from accent fabric A:

1 rectangle measuring 6" × 20"
(15 × 51 cm) for the skirt pleat

1 rectangle measuring 2" × 11"
(5 × 28 cm) for the bib pleat

2 rectangles measuring 2" × 6½"
(5 × 16.5 cm) for the pocket pleats

Cut from accent fabric B:

1 rectangle measuring 33" × 2½"
(84 × 6.5 cm) for the front waistband

4 rectangles measuring 2" × 25"
(5 × 63.5 cm) for the waist ties

4 rectangles measuring 2" × 22"
(5 × 56 cm) for the neck ties

Using the pattern, also cut from accent fabric B:

2 Pocket Half pieces

2 reversed Pocket Half pieces

Cut from the facing fabric:

1 rectangle measuring 33" × 2½"
(84 × 6.5 cm) for the waistband facing

1 full bib facing piece*

2 full pocket facing pieces*

*These will be cut later during assembly using sewn sections as patterns.

Cut from interfacing:

1 rectangle measuring 33" × 2½"
(84 × 6.5 cm) for the front waistband

A Note about Inverted Pleats

The Make & Bake Apron features inverted pleat details at the bib, the skirt, and the pockets. Each pleat has the ability to expand, providing a peek of color and ease of fit. The effect is a slightly tailored style that's not so ruffly and flouncy like some aprons.

Assemble the Skirt

Unless otherwise noted, sew all seams with a ¼" (6 mm) seam allowance.

1 Layer the skirt pleat piece on top of one of the skirt pieces, right sides together. Align and pin one set of 20" (51 cm) long edges and sew together.

Repeat, sewing the second skirt piece to the other 20" (51 cm) long edge of the skirt pleat piece. Press seams open **(figure 1)**.

2 Double hem the remaining 20" (51 cm) side edge of one of the skirt pieces. Fold in a ¼" (6 mm) hem toward the wrong side and sew, then turn in a second ¼" (6 mm) and sew.

Repeat, double hemming the 20" (51 cm) side edge of the opposite skirt piece.

3 Hem the bottom edge of the apron skirt by turning up and pressing a ¼" (6 mm) hem toward the wrong side and sewing it ⅛" (3 mm) from the edge. Turn the hem up again, this time ⅝" (1.5 cm), and sew ½" (1.3 cm) from the fold.

4 Edgestitch the skirt pleat. Fold back on itself one of the seams made in Step 1 and press. Stitch ⅛" (3 mm) from the edge through both the skirt pleat and one of the skirt pieces. This will make the edge of the skirt pleat crisp **(figure 2)**.

Repeat, edgestitching the other seam of the skirt pleat and skirt piece.

5 From the right side of the skirt, bring the two pleat seams together. Match the seams in the middle of the skirt pleat to create a reverse pleat. Press and pin so that the seams are butted together at the top edge of the skirt. Stitch across the top ³⁄₁₆" (5 mm) from the edge to secure the pleat position **(figure 3)**.

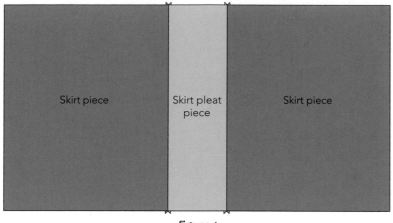

| Skirt piece | Skirt pleat piece | Skirt piece |

figure 1

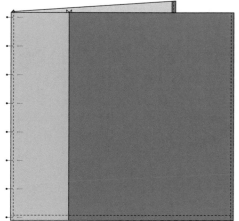

figure 2

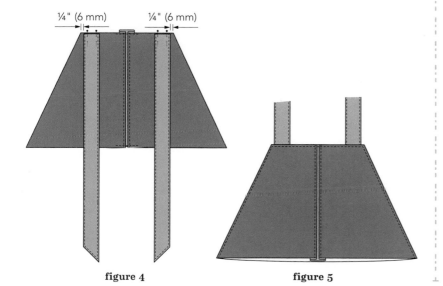

figure 3

¼" (6 mm)   ¼" (6 mm)

figure 4

figure 5

Assemble the Bib

6 Layer the bib pleat on top of one of the Apron Bib pieces, right sides together. Align one pleat edge with the center edge of the bib and sew with a ¼" (6 mm) seam allowance.

Repeat, sewing the second Apron Bib piece to the other edge of the bib pleat.

7 Edgestitch the bib pleat by folding one of the seams back on itself and pressing. Stitch ⅛" (3 mm) from the edge through both the bib pleat and one of the Apron Bib pieces.

Repeat, edgestitching the other seam of the bib pleat and the second Apron Bib piece.

Create a reverse pleat using the same process as in Step 4. Stitch across the top and bottom of the bib ³⁄₁₆" (5 mm) from the edge to secure the pleat position.

8 Layer two neck tie pieces right sides together. Cut one set of ends at a 45-degree angle. Sew together, starting at the squared end. Sew to the point of the angle, pivot, then sew back down the other edge. Turn right side out by pushing a turning tool in at the point and working the tie right side out. Press seams out, then edgestitch the perimeter of the tie ⅛" (3 mm) from the edge.

Repeat, sewing the other two neck tie pieces together in the same manner.

9 Use the sewn bib as a template to create the bib facing. Trace it onto a piece of facing fabric, then cut it out.

10 With the bib facing right side up, layer the two neck ties on top of the bib. Align the square ends of the neck ties to the top edge of the bib and pin ¼" (6 mm) from the corner **(figure 4)**. Layer the bib facing on top of the bib, right sides together, sandwiching the neck ties between layers, and pin.

Sew the bib and bib facing together along the sides and top edges, taking care to only sew over the neck ties at the top edge of the bib. Clip the seam allowance corners, turn the bib right side out, and press the seams. Edgestitch the bib ⅛" (3 mm) from the edge **(figure 5)**.

Assemble the Waist

11 Fuse the front waistband interfacing to the wrong side of the front waistband. Place the waistband facing on your work surface with the right side facing up. Layer the skirt on top, right side up. Layer the front waistband on top of the skirt, wrong side up. Align all of the top edges and center the skirt so that there is about 1" (2.5 cm) of excess waistband facing and front waistband at either end of the skirt. Sew together along the top edge with a ¼" (6 mm) seam allowance **(figure 6)**.

12 Sew the waist ties by following the same process used for the neck ties in Step 8.

13 Sandwich one of the waist ties between the right sides of the front waistband and the waistband facing, aligning the end edges **(figure 7)**. Pin into place and sew across the end with a ¼" (6 mm) seam allowance.

Turn at the bottom corner ¼" (6 mm) away from the edge and sew about 1" (2.5 cm) along the edge of the front waistband. Be sure that once you have turned the corner you are not sewing through the tie, only the front waistband and waistband facing **(figure 8)**.

Repeat on the other side with the second waist tie.

14 Clip the corners of the seam allowances and pull the ties to turn the waistband ends right side out. Press, working out the corners with a turning tool.

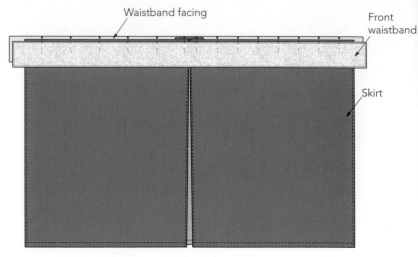

Waistband facing

Front waistband

Skirt

figure 6

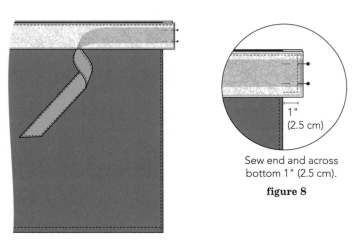

figure 7

1" (2.5 cm)

Sew end and across bottom 1" (2.5 cm).

figure 8

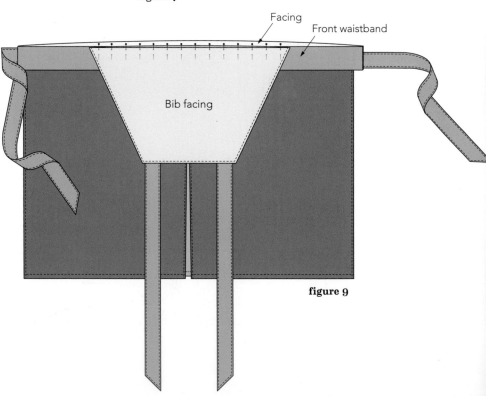

Facing

Front waistband

Bib facing

figure 9

15 Center the bib, right side down, on top of the front waistband, right sides together. Take care to align the center of the bib pleat with the center of the skirt pleat. Pin the edge of the bib to the top edge of the front waistband only and sew **(figure 9)**.

16 Flip the bib up. Press the bib seam allowances and the remaining front waistband seam allowance ¼" (6 mm) down toward the wrong side of the front waistband.

17 Across the top unsewn edge of the waistband facing, press a ¼" (6 mm) hem toward the wrong side. Press the facing into place across the back waistline of the apron and pin together through all layers, inserting the pins from the front waistband. Topstitch the entire perimeter from the front ⅛" (3 mm) from the edge, catching the waistband facing on the back.

Sew the Pockets

18 Layer the pocket pleat on top of one of the pocket pieces, right sides together, aligned with the center edge. Sew with a ¼" (6 mm) seam allowance.

Repeat, sewing the second pocket piece to the other edge of the pocket pleat.

19 Edgestitch the pocket pleat by folding one of the seams back on itself

and pressing. Stitch ⅛" (3 mm) from the edge through both the pocket pleat and one of the pocket pieces.

Repeat, edgestitching the other seam of the pocket pleat and pocket.

20 Create a reverse pleat using the same process as in Step 5. Stitch across the top and bottom of the pocket ⅛" (3 mm) from each edge to secure the pleat position.

21 Use the sewn pocket as a template to create the pocket facing. Trace it onto a piece of facing fabric, then cut it out.

22 Pin the pocket facing on top of the pocket, right sides together. Sew together, leaving 2" (5 cm) open on one side for turning. Notch the seam allowances at the curves and turn the pocket right side out. Press the seams out, then press the seam allowance at the opening to the inside. Topstitch ¼" (6 mm) from the edge across the top edge of the pocket.

Repeat the process for the second pocket.

23 Place one pocket on the front of the apron skirt, measuring 4½" (11.5 cm) down from the bottom edge of the waistband and 5½" (14 cm) over from the side hem. Pin into place. Edgestitch ⅛" (3 mm) around the sides and bottom of the pocket, leaving the top open.

Repeat for the second pocket on the opposite side of the front of the apron skirt.

stitched with meaning
transform a vintage sheet into a retro-modern apron

For an alternate fabric choice with a fun retro vibe, repurpose a bold vintage sheet for the main fabric of the apron. Many bed linens from the '70s are made with a cotton-poly blend that sheds wrinkles, making them a versatile choice for an apron.

cluck *the* chicken
{ doorstop }

finished size
10" × 14" × 5" (25.5 × 35.5 × 12.5 cm)

what you'll need

Cluck the Chicken Doorstop patterns on side D of the insert

¼ yd (23 cm) of 45" (114.5 cm) wide main fabric for the body

¼ yd (23 cm) of white wool-blend felt for the head and wings

5" × 7" (12.5 × 18 cm) piece of red wool-blend felt for the comb and wattle

3" × 3" (7.5 × 7.5 cm) square of yellow wool-blend felt for the beak

12" × 24" (30.5 × 61 cm) piece of batting

Coordinating thread

2 black buttons, ⅜" (1 cm) in diameter, for the eyes

Your sewing box

Polyester stuffing

Embroidery scissors

Handsewing needle

Pinking shears

2 quart-size zipper plastic bags

2 lb of pea gravel, aquarium pebbles, or sand

There are many questions in life about chickens, such as, "Why did the chicken cross the road?" and "Which came first, the chicken or the egg?" I don't know the answer to either, but Cluck the Chicken Doorstop is my answer to cute home décor with a good solid function. I imagine this hefty hen at home in a retro kitchen alongside vintage Pyrex and kitschy calendar tea towels, keeping the door propped open in style. The next time you need a unique housewarming gift, don't run around like a chicken with its head—well, you know. Sew up this sweet little chickie instead!

prepare materials

Using the patterns, cut from the main fabric and from the batting:

1 Body

1 reversed Body

1 Belly

Using the patterns, cut from the white felt:

2 Head pieces

4 Wings

2 Tails

Using the patterns, cut from the red felt:

2 Combs

2 Wattles

Using the pattern, cut from the yellow felt:

2 Beaks

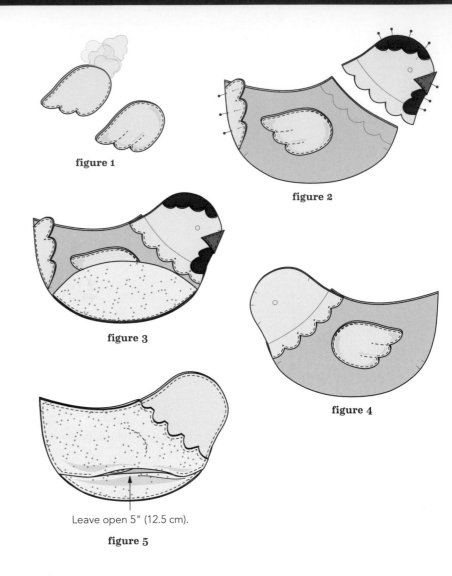

figure 1

figure 2

figure 3

figure 4

Leave open 5" (12.5 cm).

figure 5

Prepare the Body Pieces

1 Pin the cut Body and Belly pieces of batting onto the wrong sides of the main fabric Body and Belly pieces. Set aside.

Sew the Wings, Comb, Tail, Wattle, and Beak

2 Pin a pair of Wing pieces together. Using a ⅛" (3 mm) seam allowance, topstitch around the perimeter of the wing, stitching slowly and following the edges. Leave 2" (5 cm) of the curved edge open. Stuff the wing with a few pinches of polyester stuffing, then topstitch the opening closed.

Topstitch two curved lines into the wing, starting between the scallops **(figure 1)**.

Repeat to make the second wing.

3 Layer a pair of Comb pieces and topstitch ⅛" (3 mm) from the edge around the perimeter, stitching slowly and following the curves. Leave the nonscalloped edge unstitched.

4 Repeat Step 3 for the Tail pieces, Wattle pieces, and Beak pieces. Leave one straight edge open.

5 Following the placement markings on the templates, pin the tail and wing onto the main Body piece (with batting) into position. Machine baste the tail to the Body piece ⅛" (3 mm) from the edge of the tail.

Topstitch around the curve of the wing closest to the head, following the previous stitch line to secure it to the Body piece.

6 Pin the comb onto one Head piece, aligning the edges and easing the unsewn edge of the comb to match the curve of the Head piece.

Repeat for the beak and wattle (figure 2). Machine baste each piece ⅛" (3 mm) from the edge of the Head piece.

Attach the Belly and the Head to the Body

7 Pin the Belly (with batting) piece to the Body piece, right sides together, along the bottom edge. Starting and stopping ¼" (6 mm) from each end, sew together with a ¼" (6 mm) seam allowance from one point of the Belly piece to the other point.

8 Using the pattern markings as your guide, overlap the scallops of one Head piece onto the right side of one Body piece and pin along the edge. Edgestitch ⅛" (3 mm) from the scalloped edge of the head, attaching it to the body (figure 3).

9 From the back, carefully trim away the excess fabric and batting inside the scalloped stitching.

10 Repeat Step 8, layering the second Head piece onto the second Body piece. Place the second wing onto the second Body piece and stitch it in place as done in Step 5 (figure 4).

11 With a needle and thread, sew a button eye on each side of the head, following the placement marked on the pattern.

Assemble the Chicken

12 Place the body and head pieces right sides together, aligning the head and the back edges. Tuck the tail down and pin it out of the way of the seam allowances.

Pin the unsewn edge of the belly to the unsewn edge of the second Body piece. Sew around the perimeter of the chicken, leaving 5" (12.5 cm) open along the bottom edge (figure 5).

13 Trim the curved edges with pinking shears and carefully notch the seam allowances with the tips of a pair of sharp shears. Trim the corner off of the seam allowance at the tail and at the two ends of the Belly piece.

14 Turn the chicken right side out through the opening and work out the seam allowances with your fingers. Lightly press if needed.

15 Using small amounts of polyester stuffing at a time, stuff the chicken. Begin with the tail and the head. Continue to fill the body near the back.

16 Put one zipper plastic bag inside another. Fill the inner bag with pea gravel, aquarium pebbles, or sand. Press out as much air as possible and zip both inner and outer bags. Put the weight inside the chicken and continue to fill in with stuffing.

17 Fold in the seam allowances along the edge of the opening and pin the opening shut. Using a needle and thread, ladder stitch the opening closed (see Techniques, page 154).

stitched with meaning
repurpose a vintage tea towel into a decorative doorstop

Cluck the Chicken Doorstop would look adorable in the kitchen made up in a cute vintage tea towel. There are so many fun patterns and prints to match any décor, and a tea towel is just the right size for a smaller project like this.

market { shopper }

finished size
13½" × 7½" × 9½"
(34.5 × 19 × 24 cm)

what you'll need

⅔ yd (61 cm) of canvas, twill, or another midweight fabric for the exterior

½ yd (45.5 cm) of canvas, twill, or another midweight fabric for the exterior pocket

⅔ yd (61 cm) of lining fabric

1½ yd (1.4 m) of 20" (51 cm) wide woven-cotton fusible interfacing

18" × 58" (45.5 × 147.5 cm) piece of ByAnnie's Soft and Stable foam stabilizer

⅓ yd (30.5 cm) of 45" (114.5 cm) wide fusible fleece

Coordinating thread

Two 36" (91.5 cm) long pieces of 1" (2.5 cm) wide cotton webbing

Four 1" (2.5 cm) grommets

3½" (9 cm) length of hook-and-loop tape (optional)

Your sewing box

Small, sharp scissors

Dritz Fray Check

Small binding clips (optional)

Farmer's market? Flea market? I'm there! Whether it's fresh produce or vintage tchotchkes, to me there's nothing more fun to do on Saturday morning than stroll the aisles, chat with vendors, and find the perfect tomato . . . or teacup! The Market Shopper is a terrific bag to have along on such an outing. Part basket, part tote, it has a wide opening and sides that stand up. There's plenty of room on the inside and extra pockets around the outside. It even has a padded strap wrap that keeps the handles together and helps out with heavier loads. Stitch up the Market Shopper, fill it with goodies, and you'll have a thoughtful house-warming gift that anyone would love to receive.

prepare materials

Cut from the exterior fabric:

2 rectangles measuring 22" × 14½"
(56 × 37 cm) for the bag

Cut from the exterior pocket fabric:

2 rectangles measuring 22" × 11"
(56 × 28 cm) for the pocket

Cut from the lining:

2 rectangles measuring 22" × 14½"
(56 × 37 cm) for the bag

2 rectangles measuring 22" × 11"
(56 × 28 cm) for the exterior pocket

1 strip measuring 2" × 45" (5 × 114.5 cm)
for the exterior pocket binding

2 rectangles measuring 13" × 7"
(33 × 18 cm) for the interior pocket

2 squares measuring 5" × 5" (12.5 ×
12.5 cm) for the strap wrap (optional)

Cut from the fusible interfacing:

2 rectangles measuring 22" × 14½"
(56 × 37 cm) for the lining

Cut from the foam stabilizer:

2 rectangles measuring 22" × 14½"
(56 × 37 cm) for the bag

1 square measuring 5" × 5" (12.5 ×
12.5 cm) for the strap wrap (optional)

Cut from the fusible fleece:

2 rectangles measuring 22" × 11"
(56 × 28 cm) for the exterior pocket

Interface the Lining

1 Fuse the interfacing rectangles to the wrong side of the 22" × 14½" (56 × 37 cm) interior lining rectangles. Measure, mark, and cut away a 4" × 4" (10 × 10 cm) square from the bottom two corners of each of the lining, stabilizer, and exterior rectangles (**figure 1**).

2 Following the manufacturer's instructions, fuse the fusible fleece rectangles to the wrong side of the 22" × 11" (56 × 28 cm) exterior pocket rectangles. Measure, mark, and cut away a 4" × 4" (10 × 10 cm) square from the bottom two corners of each of the exterior pocket and pocket lining rectangles (as in **figure 1**).

Sew the Exterior Pocket

3 Layer the two exterior pocket pieces right sides together and sew each side seam with a ¼" (6 mm) seam allowance. Press seams open.

Repeat the process for the two exterior pocket lining pieces.

4 With wrong sides together, place the exterior pocket lining inside the exterior pocket. Align the side seams and pin the top edges. Sew the two layers together around the top ⅛" (3 mm) from the edge.

5 Fold the binding strip in half lengthwise and press. Open, then fold one raw edge in toward the center fold and press again. Fold the other raw edge into the center fold and press. Press one more time with all three folds encapsulating the raw edges.

6 Keeping the binding edges folded inward, open up the center fold and sandwich the top edge of the sewn exterior pocket into the binding. Align one end of the binding ¼" (6 mm) past one of the side seams. Pin the binding all the way around the top edge.

Overlap the side seam you began by ¼" (6 mm) and cut off the excess. To seam the ends of the binding together, unpin the ends of the binding from the top edge a few inches back. Match the ends of the binding, right sides together, and sew with a ¼" (6 mm) seam allowance (**figure 2**).

Refold and repin the binding to the top edge of the sewn exterior pocket. Topstitch ⅛" (3 mm) from the edge of the binding through all layers.

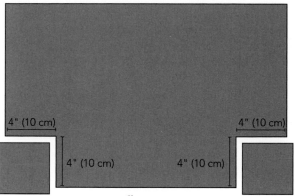

figure 1

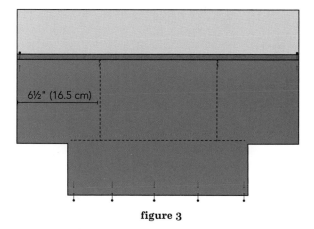

figure 2

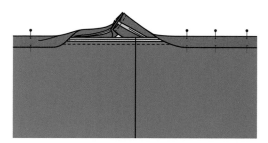

figure 3

A Note about Foam Stabilizer

ByAnnie's Soft and Stable is the perfect stabilizer for this project. It is a thin foam fused between two layers of knit fabric. It adds firm body to a project without adding a lot of weight, allowing the bag to stand up. If you have trouble locating this product, I've read that some people have used automotive headliner as a replacement.

Sew the Exterior Bag

7 Layer the two exterior bag pieces right sides together. Trim off ½" (1.3 cm) across the top of the foam stabilizer pieces, then layer them onto both of the wrong sides of the exterior bag pieces. The exterior bag pieces should be sandwiched between the foam stabilizer pieces and aligned across the bottom edges.

8 Pin and sew each side seam with a ¼" (6 mm) seam allowance through all layers, starting at the bottom of the seam and sewing up. Press seams open and trim away the foam stabilizer seam allowances to ⅛" (3 mm). Turn the exterior bag right side out.

9 Slide the sewn exterior pocket over the sewn exterior bag. The lining side of the pocket should face the right side of the exterior bag. Align and pin the side seams and the bottom edges.

10 To create pocket divisions, make two marks with a disappearing-ink fabric marker along the binding 6½" (16.5 cm) in from each side seam. With a ruler and the marker, draw a vertical line perpendicular to the binding from each mark toward the bottom of the bag. Draw another line across the bottom of the pocket ¼" (6 mm) above the corner cutouts, stopping ¼" (6 mm) from the corners.

Topstitch the front of the exterior pocket to the front of the exterior bag along the markings, backstitching at the top of the pocket for reinforcement **(figure 3)**.

11 Turn the exterior bag over and mark and sew the exterior pocket divisions on the back of the bag in the same fashion.

12 Turn the exterior bag inside out. Align and pin the bottom edges between the corner cutouts. Sew with a ¼" (6 mm) seam allowance through all layers. Trim away the foam stabilizer seam allowance to ⅛" (3 mm) to reduce bulk.

13 Pinch the corners together by matching the side seam to the bottom seam and flattening the bag. Pin the layers together, then sew with a ¼" (6 mm) seam allowance. Trim away the foam stabilizer seam allowance again. Turn the bag right side out and press.

Sew the Bag Lining

14 Pin the two interior pocket pieces right sides together. Sew around the perimeter with a ¼" (6 mm) seam allowance, leaving a 3" (7.5 cm) opening for turning. Clip the seam allowances at the corners, turn right side out, and press, working out the corners with a turning tool. Press the seam allowances in at the opening.

Topstitch across the top edge of the pocket ¼" (6 mm) from the edge.

15 Pin the sewn pocket on top of the back interior lining piece, right sides up, 3" (7.5 cm) from the top edge of the back interior lining, and centered side to side. Sew the sides and bottom with a ⅛" (3 mm) seam allowance, closing the 3" (7.5 cm) opening as you sew.

16 Mark the top center edge of the pocket with a disappearing-ink fabric marker. Sew through all layers at this mark, perpendicularly from the top edge of the pocket, to create pocket segments.

17 Layer both of the interior lining pieces right sides together. Pin the side and bottom seams and sew with a ½" (1.3 cm) seam allowance. Pinch the corners together by matching the side seam to the bottom seam and flattening the lining. Pin, then sew together with a ½" (1.3 cm) seam allowance. Press all seam allowances open.

Attach the Lining

18 Put the interior lining inside the exterior bag so that the wrong sides are facing. Work the lining corners down into the exterior bag corners. Smooth the lining with your hands and pin at the side seams and other areas to help align and situate the lining.

19 Fold the top edge of the exterior bag down toward the wrong side and pin, covering the top edge of the foam stabilizer. Continue pinning all the way around the perimeter of the bag. Fold the top edge of the lining down toward the bag exterior so it is even with the top of the bag.

As you pin the lining and the bag together, make sure that the lining is smooth. You may find that using small binding clips instead of pins

works great for this project. Finish the top edge of the bag with two rows of topstitching at ⅛" (3 mm) and ⅜" (1 cm).

Install the Grommets

20 Lay the bag flat on your work surface. Mark the first grommet placement with a tiny pencil mark that indicates the center of the grommet, 1⅝" (4 cm) down from the top edge and 6½" (16.5 cm) from the side seam of the exterior bag (above the stitched pocket division).

21 Using the circle template provided in the grommet package, mark the fabric to cut away (reference the manufacturer's instructions). Place a few straight pins around the marked circle to keep the layers from shifting. With small sharp scissors, snip a small hole through the front exterior bag and interior lining. Continue to cut away the marked circle through all layers, removing pins as you go.

22 Insert the tip of your scissors in between the layers and trim away an extra ¼" (6 mm) of the foam stabilizer. You may want to apply a little Fray Check to the cut edges of the hole if your fabrics have a loose weave.

23 The grommets have two components that snap together. Place one component into the hole from the outside of the bag. Place the opposite component into the hole from the inside of the bag. Snap the two grommet pieces together with your fingers or by pushing down with the heel of your hand onto a hard surface.

Repeat the process for the other three grommets.

Make the Handles

24 Finish the cut ends of the two 36" (91.5 cm) lengths of wide cotton webbing with a zigzag stitch in matching thread.

25 Thread one end of the webbing through a grommet from the outside of the bag toward the inside. Fold 3" to 4" (7.5 to 10 cm) of the webbing back onto itself and pin. Sew a 1" (2.5 cm) wide square through both layers.

Repeat for the other end of the strap on the same side of the bag, taking care not to twist the strap.

Attach the second strap to the other side of the bag in the same way.

Make the Optional Strap Wrap

26 Pin the two 5" (12.5 cm) squares of lining fabric, right sides together, onto the 5" (12.5 cm) square of foam stabilizer. Sew around the perimeter with a ¼" (6 mm) seam allowance, leaving a 2" (5 cm) opening on one side for turning.

Trim the seam allowances to ⅛" (3 mm)—except for the lining fabric at the opening—and turn the square right side out so that the foam stabilizer is sandwiched between the lining pieces. Press, turning in the seam allowances at the opening, and pin. Edgestitch the perimeter ⅛" (3 mm) from the edge.

27 Separate the 3½" (9 cm) piece of hook-and-loop tape. Pin one side of the tape ¼" (6 mm) from one end of the square and topstitch. Pin the other side of the tape to the back of the square at the other end and topstitch **(figure 4)**. Wrap the piece around both straps to hold them together.

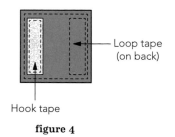

Loop tape (on back)

Hook tape

figure 4

stitched with meaning
turn a retro tablecloth into a one-of-a-kind tote

A retired tablecloth can get a second life as the outer fabric of the Market Shopper, making a one-of-a-kind tote. Choose one that's a sturdy home-dec weight. Be sure to navigate around any holes or stains when cutting out your pieces.

hot mitt *house*

{ & tea towel set }

finished size

Hot Mitt: 8" × 11" (20.5 × 28 cm)

Tea Towel: 15" × 24" (38 × 61 cm)

what you'll need

Hot Mitt House & Tea Towel Set patterns on side D of the insert

½ yd (45.5 cm) of white linen or cotton huck toweling

¼ yd (23 cm) of printed quilting cotton for the main fabric

¼ yd (23 cm) of printed quilting cotton for the lining

½ yd (45.5 cm) of heat-resistant batting

10 small scraps of printed quilting cottons for the appliqués

8½" × 11" (21.5 × 28 cm) sheet of double-sided fusible webbing

Coordinating thread

Coordinating embroidery floss and needle

1 package of extra-wide double-fold bias binding

1 small and 1 large button

Your sewing box

Rotary cutter, self-healing mat, and ruler

Handsewing needle

To a newcomer on your block, a handmade house-warming gift says, "Welcome to the neighborhood. We're glad you're here!" The Hot Mitt House & Tea Towel Set is an adorable way to share that friendly sentiment. The appliquéd details are easily customizable, and the premade binding helps this project come together in a snap. Have fun mixing and matching prints, or put some pretty scraps from your stash to good use.

prepare materials for the Hot Mitt House

Using the patterns, cut from the main fabric:

1 Front

1 Roof

1 Back

Using the patterns as a reference, cut pieces from the lining fabric 1" (2.5 cm) larger in each direction:

1 Front

1 Roof

1 Back

Using the patterns as a reference, cut pieces from the insulated batting 1" (2.5 cm) larger in each direction:

1 Front

1 Roof

2 Back pieces

Use a pencil to trace the appliqué patterns onto the fusible webbing, then loosely cut around the pencil lines:

1 Door

1 Window

2 Shutter pieces

1 Bird

prepare materials for the Tea Towel

From the linen or cotton huck toweling, cut:

1 rectangle measuring 16" × 25" (40.5 × 63.5 cm)

From the lining fabric scraps, cut:

2 strips measuring 1½" × 15½" (3.8 × 39.5 cm) for the hem

Use a pencil to trace the appliqué patterns onto the fusible webbing, then loosely cut around the pencil lines:

9 Little House Appliqués

Build the Hot Mitt House

1 Following the manufacturer's instructions, fuse each piece of fusible webbing to the wrong side of the appliqué quilting fabric scraps. Cut out each shape directly on the pencil line and peel off the paper backing.

2 Place the Roof lining piece, right side down, onto your work surface. Layer the Roof batting on top, then center the main Roof piece right side up on top of the batting. Pin layers together into a sandwich.

3 Repeat this for the Front pieces and for the Back pieces of the house, including both layers of batting.

Quilt in Two Directions

4 With a disappearing-ink fabric marker, measure and mark a vertical line every 1" (2.5 cm) on each of the main fabric pieces. Next, mark a line every 1" (2.5 cm) at an angle that matches the slope of the roof, using the Roof pattern as a guide.

5 Install a walking foot on your machine if you have one. Quilt through all layers by topstitching on the drawn lines, starting from the center of each sandwich (**figure 1**).

After the house pieces are quilted, use a ruler and rotary cutter to even up the edges and trim away the excess batting and lining.

Appliqué the Details

6 Place the Door, Window, and Shutter appliqués right side up on the right side of the front of the house. Cover with a press cloth and iron, fusing each piece to the main fabric.

7 Using a machine blanket stitch or another decorative stitch, sew around each shape. Following the pattern, mark windowpanes with a disappearing-ink fabric marker and stitch.

8 After adding the panes, fuse the bird on top. Embroider the bird details: one French knot or tiny stitch for the eye, a single running stitch for the beak, and a single chain stitch for the wing (see Techniques, page 154, for embroidery techniques).

Sew a button for the doorknob onto the door and another accent button onto the roof, if desired.

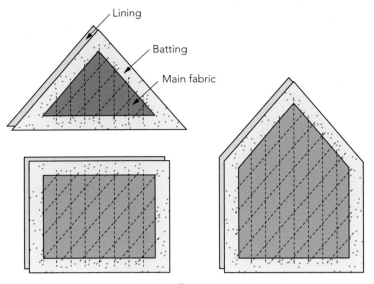

- Lining
- Batting
- Main fabric

figure 1

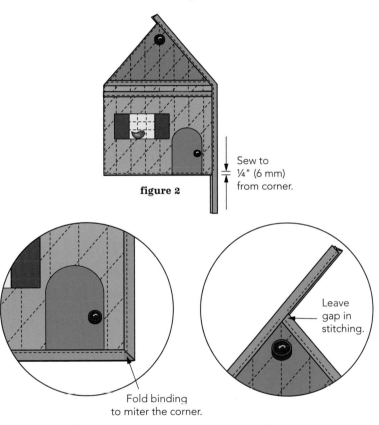

Sew to
¼" (6 mm)
from corner.

figure 2

Fold binding
to miter the corner.

figure 3

Leave
gap in
stitching.

figure 4

A Note about Batting

The Hot Mitt uses heat-resistant batting, such as The Warm Company's Insul-Brite, to protect your hand from the heat of your oven. It's a special insulating batting with a layer of Mylar inside that can withstand high temperatures.

Layer and Bind the House

9 Open up the double-fold binding and find one end. Sandwich the bottom edge of the roof into the center fold of the binding. Pin or use quilter's binding clips to hold the binding in place. Sew the binding through all layers about ⅜" (1 cm) from the outside fold of the binding. Trim off the excess binding.

Repeat this step for the top edge of the house front.

10 Layer the roof and front on top of the back of the house with the lining sides together. Pin around the perimeter, then machine baste the roof and the front to the back of the house ⅛" (3 mm) from the outside edge.

11 Starting at the point of the roof, sandwich the staystitched layers into the center fold of the binding, pinning or clipping to hold the binding in place. Ease the binding around the turn where the bottom of the roof meets the front of the house, then continue sandwiching the edges down to the bottom corner of the front.

12 Sew the binding through all layers about ⅜" (1 cm) from the outside fold of the binding (about ⅛" [3 mm] from the inside edge of the binding), stopping about ¼" (6 mm) from the bottom corner of the front (**figure 2**).

13 At the bottom corner, remove the work from your sewing machine. Fold the binding at a right angle, mitering it at the corner (**figure 3**).

Repin or clip the binding and continue sandwiching and sewing the binding in place. Miter the second front corner and continue attaching the binding up to the point of the roof. Stop stitching at the point before the binding overlaps.

Create the Loop

14 Leave a 5" (12.5 cm) tail of binding, then cut off the rest. Continue the topstitching on the tail, starting just past the point where the binding overlaps. Leave a small gap in the stitching (**figure 4**).

15 Fold back the cut end of the binding and tuck it into the gap. Complete the line of topstitching, closing the gap and catching the end of the binding **(figure 5)** to make the loop.

Secure the loop by topstitching across the point of the roof **(figure 6)**.

Make the Tea Towel

16 Begin the towel by folding over a ¼" (6 mm) hem along the long sides of the cotton rectangle and press. Fold the hem over again and stitch ¼" (6 mm) from the edge.

17 Layer one strip of lining fabric, right side down, onto the right side of the towel, aligning the raw edges with ¼" (6 mm) of excess fabric extending at each end. Sew together ¼" (6 mm) from the raw edge.

18 Fold the accent strip down at the seam and press **(figure 7)**. Turn the towel wrong side up, then fold the ends of the contrast strip in and press **(figure 8)**.

Press a ¼" (6 mm) hem along the raw edge of the contrast strip toward the wrong side of the towel **(figure 9)**.

Fold the strip lengthwise, aligning the folded hem with the contrast strip seam line **(figure 10)**. Pin and topstitch from the right side of the towel ⅛" (3 mm) from the seam line and across the ends.

19 Repeat this step to apply the contrast strip on the other end of the towel.

Appliqué the Little Houses

20 Using an iron and following the manufacturer's instructions, fuse each of the nine pieces of webbing to the wrong side of the various appliqué fabric scraps. Cut out each Little House Appliqué directly on the pencil line and peel off the paper backing.

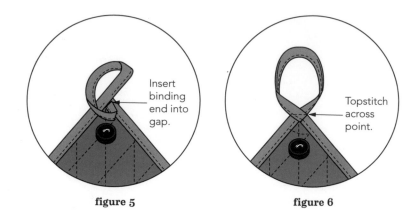

figure 5   figure 6

figure 7

figure 8

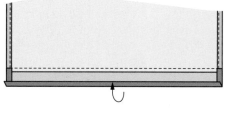

figure 9

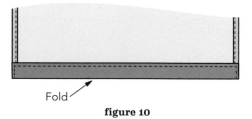

figure 10

21 With a disappearing-ink fabric marker, draw a line across the bottom edge of the towel ½" (1.3 cm) up from one of the sewn contrast strips.

22 Center one house appliqué on the line and then place the others next to it on either side. Cover with a press cloth and fuse to the towel.

Using a machine blanket stitch or another decorative stitch, sew around each shape.

23 With a needle and embroidery floss, embroider a running stitch (see Techniques, page 154) across the houses at the bottom of the roof line. Knot the embroidery floss on the back and trim.

stitched with meaning
turn a plaid shirt into a festive holiday Hot Mitt House

For an alternative look and a specific season, make the Hot Mitt House in holiday fabrics. Repurpose a plaid shirt and trim it with red or white binding for a gingerbread house hot mitt. Repeat your fabric choices in the tea towel appliqués to coordinate.

it's your
pot-lucky day
{ casserole caddy }

finished size

10" × 16" (25.5 × 40.5 cm), which fits a 9" × 13" (23 × 33 cm) casserole dish with handles

what you'll need

It's Your Pot-Lucky Day: Casserole Caddy patterns on side C of the insert

½ yd (45.5 cm) of 45" (114.5 cm) wide main fabric A for caddy bottom

½ yd (45.5 cm) of 45" (114.5 cm) wide main fabric B for caddy lid and sides

½ yd (45.5 cm) of 45" (114.5 cm) wide lining fabric

Coordinating thread

2 yd (1.8 m) of 20" (51 cm) wide woven fusible interfacing

1 yd (91.5 cm) of ByAnnie's Soft and Stable foam stabilizer

5" (12.5 cm) length of 1" (2.5 cm) wide hook-and-loop tape

Your sewing box

Glue stick (optional)

"Luck" is the key word when you are invited to a potluck dinner. It's fun to share a family favorite, plus you get to sample a bit of everyone else's specialty dishes. The only time I feel not so lucky is when it's time to transport the tasty treat. With this Casserole Caddy, there will be no more balancing a hot dish on your lap or sloshing sauce on your car's floor mats. Made up in cute picnicky prints, it says summer dining all over it. Prepare a dinner for a new mom and present it to her in a cute caddy. She'll be so happy, she might even let you hold the baby!

prepare materials

Cut from the foam stabilizer:

1 bottom base piece measuring 17½" × 10" (44.5 × 25.5 cm)

2 bottom front and back pieces measuring 3½" × 17½" (9 × 44.5 cm)

2 bottom side pieces measuring 3½" × 10" (9 × 25.5 cm)

1 lid center piece measuring 10½" × 18" (26.5 × 45.5 cm)

1 lid front piece measuring 2½" × 18" (6.5 × 45.5 cm)

Using the pattern, also cut from the foam stabilizer:

2 Lid Side pieces

Cut from main fabric A, interfacing, and lining fabric:

1 bottom base piece measuring 17½" × 10" (44.5 × 25.5 cm)

2 bottom front and back pieces measuring 4" × 17½" (10 × 44.5 cm)

2 bottom side pieces measuring 4" × 10" (10 × 25.5 cm)

From main fabric A, also cut:

2 hinge pieces 1" × 16½" (2.5 × 42 cm)

Cut from main fabric B, interfacing, and lining:

1 lid center piece measuring 11" × 18" (28 × 45.5 cm)

1 lid front piece measuring 3" × 18" (7.5 × 45.5 cm)

Using the pattern, also cut from main fabric B, interfacing, and lining:

1 Lid Side

1 reversed Lid Side

From the lining, cut:

2 strap pieces measuring 4" × 38" (10 × 96.5 cm)

Fuse the Interfacing

1 Fuse interfacing to the wrong sides of all of the pieces cut from main fabric A and main fabric B.

Sew the Lining and Foam Bottom

All of the foam and lining seam allowances are ¼" (6 mm). All of the main fabric A and main fabric B seam allowances are ⅛" (3 mm).

2 Layer the wrong side of the bottom base lining on top of the bottom base foam stabilizer. Layer the wrong side of the bottom front lining on top of the bottom front foam stabilizer, aligning one set of long edges. The lining piece will extend ½" (1.3 cm) above the edge of the foam.

3 Layer those pieces, right sides together, on top of one long edge of the bottom base lining and foam. Pin the edges. Sew, starting and stopping ¼" (6 mm) from the beginning and end of the seam (**figure 1**).

4 Repeat this process, sewing the bottom back lining and foam stabilizer and the bottom side lining and foam stabilizer to the bottom base lining and foam stabilizer (**figure 2**). Carefully and as evenly as possible, trim away the excess seam allowances to about ⅛" (3 mm).

5 With right sides together, pin a set of ends together at one corner of the bottom base. Sew through all layers.

Repeat for the three other corners. Trim the seam allowances to ⅛" (3 mm).

Sew the Exterior Bottom

6 Layer the exterior bottom front on top of one long edge of the exterior bottom base, right sides together, and pin the edges. Sew with a ⅛" (3 mm) seam allowance, starting and stopping ⅛" (3 mm) from the beginning and end of the seam.

7 Repeat this process to sew the exterior bottom back and both exterior bottom side pieces. Press seam allowances open.

8 With right sides together, align, pin and sew a set of ends together at the corner of the exterior bottom base.

Repeat for the three other corners. Press the seam allowances open.

A Note about Foam Stabilizer

ByAnnie's Soft and Stable foam stabilizer is what gives this project its body and helps the caddy stand up. It's not difficult to work with, but it does require a little extra care and maneuvering when sewing.

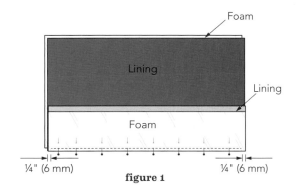

figure 1

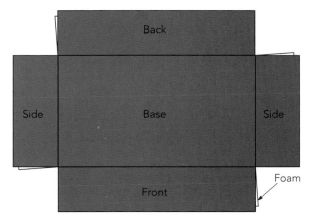

figure 2

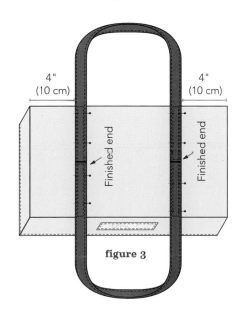

figure 3

9 With wrong sides facing, place the lining and foam bottom inside the sewn exterior bottom, aligning the seams and corners. The foam stabilizer will be sandwiched between the lining and exterior fabric. Fold the lining edges that extend above the top edge of the foam down to the outside of the foam and pin. Evenly fold the main fabric toward the foam and pin along the top edges.

Topstitch the front and two sides ⅛" (3 mm) from the edge. Leave the back pinned and unsewn.

10 Separate the two sides of the hook-and-loop tape strip. Place one piece on the outside of the exterior bottom front, ¾" (2 cm) down from the top edge and centered side to side.

Because hook-and-loop tape is difficult to pin through, try using a glue stick to hold it in place.

Topstitch around the perimeter ⅛" (3 mm) from the edge through all layers.

Sew and Attach the Straps

11 Fold one of the strap pieces lengthwise and press to create a crease that runs the length of the rectangle. Open the fold, then fold the side edges into the center crease and press.

12 Open the folds again, then fold in one short end ¼" (6 mm) and press, taking care not to erase the previous creases. Refold the lengthwise folds so that the raw edges are all enclosed except for one unfinished end of that strap.

Topstitch both side edges and the finished end of the strap at ⅛" (3 mm).

13 Repeat Steps 11 and 12 to create the second strap.

14 With a disappearing-ink fabric marker, measure and mark the exterior bottom base at the front and back edges 4" (10 cm) from the sides. Draw a line from the front markings to the back markings. Find the center point of each line and make another small mark. These will be your guides for the strap placement.

15 Place the unfinished end of one strap at the center mark on one line. Pin the strap in place along the base to the edge of the exterior bottom base. Pin the other end of that strap to the center mark on the other line.

it's your pot-lucky day { casserole caddy } **133**

Repeat with the second strap, aligning the ends of the strap with the center and pinning.

16 Repin the ends of the straps so that each finished end is on top of the unfinished ends. Topstitch to the bottom base through all layers, following the previous topstitching on the straps and crossing the strap at the front and back edges of the base (**figure 3**, page 133).

Sew the Caddy Lid

17 Layer the wrong side of the lid center lining on top of the lid center foam piece. Layer the wrong side of the lid front lining on top of the lid front foam piece, aligning one set of long edges. The lining piece will extend ½" (1.3 cm) above the edge of the foam.

Now layer those, right sides together, on top of one long edge of the lid center lining and foam panel and pin the edges. Sew together, starting and stopping ¼" (6 mm) from the beginning and end of the seam.

18 Repeat this process for both of the Lid Side lining pieces and Lid Side foam stabilizer pieces. Trim away the excess seam allowances to about ⅛" (3 mm).

19 With right sides together, align, pin, and sew a set of ends together at the corner of the lid center.

Repeat for the other corner, then trim the seam allowances to ⅛" (3 mm).

20 Place the matching piece of the hook-and-loop tape strip to the inside of the lid front lining ¾" (2 cm) down from the top sewn edge and centered side to side. Topstitch around the perimeter ⅛" (3 mm) from the edge.

21 Layer the exterior lid front on top of one long edge of the exterior lid center, right sides together, and pin the edges. Sew together, starting and stopping ⅛" (3 mm) from the beginning and end of the seam.

22 Repeat this process for both exterior Lid Side pieces. Press the seam allowances open.

23 With right sides together, align, pin, and sew a set of ends together at the corner of the exterior lid center.

Repeat for the other corner, then press the seam allowances open.

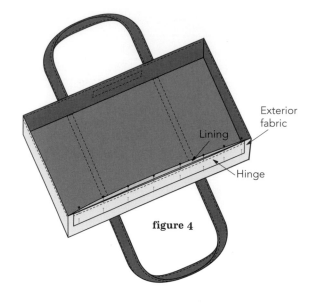

Exterior fabric
Lining
Hinge

figure 4

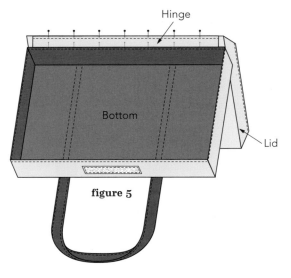

Hinge
Bottom
Lid

figure 5

24 With wrong sides facing, place the lining and foam lid inside the exterior lid, aligning the seams and corners. Fold the lining edges that extend above the top edge of the foam stabilizer down to the outside of the foam and pin. Evenly fold the main fabric toward the foam stabilizer and pin along the top edges. Continue pinning the excess down along the side panels.

Topstitch the front and two side edges at ⅛" (3 mm). Leave the back edge pinned and unsewn.

Sew the Hinge

25 Layer the two hinge pieces right sides together. Sew the short ends together, then turn right side out and press.

26 Unpin the exterior back bottom piece and align one long edge of the hinge to the back, centering and pinning it to the exterior fabric only, and sew (**figure 4**).

27 Press the seam and refold the seam allowance of the exterior back bottom back against the foam stabilizer. Repin the bottom back lining edge over the foam. Topstitch through all layers, sandwiching the hinge between the lining and foam and the exterior fabric.

28 Repeat this process by unpinning the exterior center lid piece and aligning the raw edge of the hinge to the lid, centering and pinning it to the exterior fabric only, and sew (**figure 5**).

29 Press the seam and refold the seam allowance of the exterior center lid back against the foam stabilizer. Repin the center lid lining edge over the foam. Topstitch through all layers, sandwiching the hinge between the lining and foam stabilizer and the exterior fabric.

stitched with meaning
upcycle a laminated tablecloth for a wipe-clean caddy

Try making your Casserole Caddy with a picnic tablecloth as the exterior. One that's vinyl or laminated cotton will wipe clean with a damp cloth. Stitching on sticky fabrics can be a challenge, so be sure to practice on scraps. A piece of clear tape on the bottom of your presser foot (leaving a hole for the needle to go through) and one on the plate next to the feed dogs can help keep vinyl moving smoothly through your sewing machine.

falling leaves
{ appliquéd placemats }

finished size
13½" × 18" (34.5 × 45.5 cm) each

what you'll need

Falling Leaves Appliquéd Placemats pattern on side C of the insert

3 yd (2.7 m) total of various prints and solid quilting cottons

1 yd (91.5 cm) of backing fabric

1 yd (91.5 cm) of batting

1½ yd (1.4 m) of fusible webbing

Coordinating or contrasting thread

Your sewing box

Rotary cutter, self-healing mat, and ruler

I'm of the attitude that one can never have too many placemats. Less formal than a tablecloth, placemats pretty up the table and give each person a space of his or her own. Each of these placemats is pieced with squares, then appliquéd and embellished with free-motion stitching. This project of four appliquéd placemats is perfect for stash busting or for using a few precut charm packs to save cutting time.

prepare materials

Cut from assorted prints and solids:
48 squares measuring 5" × 5" (12.5 × 12.5 cm) for the appliquéd leaves

Cut from the backing fabric and the batting:
4 rectangles measuring 14" × 18½" (35.5 × 47 cm)

figure 1

Trace the Leaf Appliqués

1 Using the Leaf Appliqué pattern, trace forty-eight leaves onto the fusible webbing and loosely cut them out around the traced outlines. Using an iron, fuse each piece of webbing to the wrong sides of the various prints and solids. Cut out each shape directly on the pencil line and peel off the paper backing.

Piece and Appliqué the Placemats

2 Plan the patchwork arrangement for each placemat by laying out four sets of twelve background squares, right side up, onto your work surface.

3 Lay out the leaf appliqués diagonally on top of the squares with the fusible webbing facing down **(figure 1)**. Cover each appliqué with a press cloth and fuse to the corresponding square. If desired, snap a photo of your arrangements so that once you start sewing you can refer to it.

Why not make a quick set of coordinating coasters?

To make a set of matching coasters, simply cut out and fuse additional appliqué leaves onto extra squares. Then follow Steps 6 through 8 of the placemat instructions to sew and quilt the coasters.

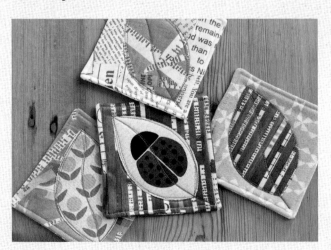

4 For the placemat top, sew the squares together with a ¼" (6 mm) seam allowance in three rows of four squares.

Press the seam allowances open, then pin the rows together. Take care to align all of the seams by placing one pin directly through each seam. Sew with a ¼" (6 mm) seam allowance and press the seam open.

5 Repeat Steps 2 through 4 to sew the other three placemats.

Quilt the Placemats

6 With the right side up, layer each placemat top onto a piece of batting and baste together with pins. Free-motion stitch around the outer edge of each leaf appliqué.

Stitch up the center of each leaf to create a stem and veins if desired. Because of the gentle curves of the leaf, this can be done on any straight stitch machine without the use of a special free motion foot.

After the decorative stitching is complete, use a ruler and rotary cutter to trim and square up the edges of each mat top.

7 Place a backing rectangle, right side up, onto your work surface. Layer a placemat top, right side down, onto the backing. Use a ruler and rotary cutter to trim the edges of the backing to match the size of the placemat top. Pin the layers together.

8 Using a ¼" (6 mm) seam allowance, sew around the perimeter of the placemat. Leave a 6" (15 cm) opening for turning along one short side. Clip the corners of the seam allowance, then turn the placemat right side out and press.

Fold the seam allowances in at the opening and pin. Topstitch around the entire placemat ⅛" (3 mm) from the edge.

9 Quilt the placemat as desired. The placemat pictured on page 136 was quilted by stitching in the ditch along each seam line of the patchwork.

10 Repeat Steps 6 through 9 to complete the other three placemats.

stitched with meaning
swap in scraps of dress shirts for mix-and-match placemats

Because this project uses many smaller pieces, it's the perfect opportunity to reuse fabrics cut from existing items. I'd love to see a more masculine set of placemats made with a variety of men's dress shirts. A combination of stripes and plaids in a cohesive color palette would be handsome. An extra bonus: Some dress shirts are treated with a stain resistant finish, which is perfect for placemats!

color-blocked
{ felt bins }

finished size

Small: 4½" × 4½" × 6"
(11.5 × 11.5 × 15 cm)

Large: 6" × 6" × 8"
(15 × 15 × 20.5 cm)

what you'll need

½ yd (45.5 cm) of 36" (91.5 cm) wide wool-blend felt color A

½ yd (45.5 cm) of 36" (91.5 cm) wide wool-blend felt color B

1 yd (91.5 cm) of 17" (43 cm) wide double-sided fusible webbing

Coordinating thread

Your sewing box

Rotary cutter, self-healing mat, and ruler

Tailor's ham or a rolled-up towel

Painter's tape (optional)

Containing clutter can be a constant battle. Get a loved one (or yourself) organized with these two fun and felty color-blocked bins. Their clean graphic look will bring calm to the chaos, providing a place to gather sewing notions, craft items, or small accessories. The two-sided felt is created with fusible webbing, which adds thickness, stability, and an extra pop of color. The unique but simple construction makes them fun to create and a joy to give.

prepare materials

To make the large color-blocked bin, cut rectangles measuring 5" × 14½" (12.5 × 37 cm):

4 from felt color A

4 from felt color B

4 from double-sided fusible webbing

To make the small color-blocked bin, cut rectangles measuring 3½" × 10" (9 × 25.5 cm):

4 from felt color A

4 from felt color B

4 from double-sided fusible webbing

To make the large striped bin, cut rectangles measuring 2½" × 14½" (6.5 × 37 cm):

4 from felt color A

4 from felt color B

4 from double-sided fusible webbing

For the large striped bin, also cut rectangles measuring 2½" × 12¼" (6.5 × 31 cm):

4 from felt color A

4 from felt color B

4 from double-sided fusible webbing

To make the small striped bin, cut rectangles measuring 1¾" × 10" (4.5 × 25.5 cm):

4 from felt color A

4 from felt color B

4 from double-sided fusible webbing

For the small striped bin, also cut rectangles measuring 1¾" × 8½" (4.5 × 21.5 cm):

4 from felt color A

4 from felt color B

4 from double-sided fusible webbing

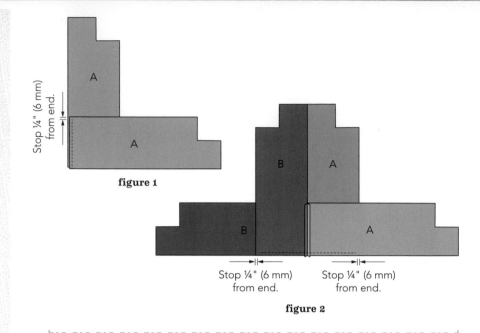

Stop ¼" (6 mm) from end.

figure 1

Stop ¼" (6 mm) from end.

Stop ¼" (6 mm) from end.

figure 2

Make the Color-Blocked Felt Bins

Follow the same steps to make both sizes of the Color-Blocked Bins.

1 Following the manufacturer's instructions, fuse a rectangle of double-sided fusible webbing to one color A felt rectangle. Peel away the paper backing and discard. Place that rectangle, webbing side down, on top of one color B felt rectangle. Cover with a press cloth and fuse the two rectangles together.

Repeat to fuse the webbing to the other three sets of felt rectangles.

2 Place one fused rectangle, with the color A side facing up, vertically on your work surface. For the large bin, measure and mark a 2¼" (5.5 cm) square in the upper right-hand corner with a disappearing-ink fabric marker. For the small bin, measure and mark a 1½" (3.8 cm) square. Cut the square away.

Repeat the process on a second rectangle, color A side up. Repeat twice on the last two rectangles with the color B side facing up.

3 Place two notched rectangles together, with a color A and a color B side facing, at the corners with the short end of one aligned with the

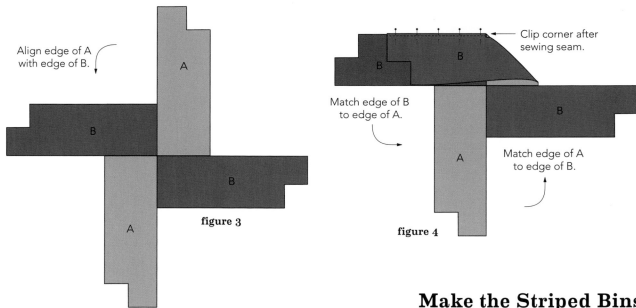

Align edge of A with edge of B.

A

B

B

A

figure 3

Clip corner after sewing seam.

B

B

B

Match edge of B to edge of A.

A

Match edge of A to edge of B.

figure 4

long side of the other. Sew together with a ¼" (6 mm) seam allowance, starting at the corner and ending ¼" (6 mm) from the end of the short side. Press the seam open (**figure 1**).

Repeat with the second pair of notched rectangles.

4 With right sides together (the sides without seam allowances), place one pair of notched rectangles on top of the other pair of notched rectangles, aligning the sewn seams and outer edges (**figure 2**).

Pin, then sew together with a ¼" (6 mm) seam allowance that starts and stops ¼" (6 mm) from the end of the seam line. Open up the work flat and press the seams lightly (**figure 3**).

5 Align the side edge of one notched rectangle with the edge of the adjacent notched rectangle, right sides together, and pin. Sew together using a ¼" (6 mm) seam allowance from beginning to end. Clip the corner seam allowance protruding from the end of the seam (**figure 4**).

Repeat this process, matching each set of adjacent sides until all four side seams are sewn.

6 Turn the felt bin right side out. Press gently, placing a tailor's ham or a rolled-up towel inside the bin.

Make the Striped Bins

7 Because you will be working with striped panels, you may want to label each side with a piece of painter's tape that designates an A side and a B side. This will help you keep them straight when following the figures.

8 Following the manufacturer's instructions, fuse a rectangle of webbing to one long color A rectangle. Peel away the paper backing and discard. Place the long color A rectangle with the webbing side down on top of a long color B rectangle. Cover with a press cloth and fuse the two long rectangles together.

Repeat for the other three sets of long rectangles and for the four sets of short color A and color B rectangles.

9 Set your sewing machine on a zigzag stitch, 5 wide and 1½ long. Align the ends of a long rectangle with the B side up and a short rectangle with the A side up side by side, butting the edges together. Zigzag stitch the edges together, letting the stitch straddle the edges where the rectangles meet (see Techniques, page 154, for sewing butted seams).

Repeat, sewing together each pair of long and short rectangles in the same color A and color B configuration for a total of four notched rectangles.

10 To finish the Striped Bins, follow the directions for the Color-Blocked Bins beginning with Step 3.

dream home
{ quilt }

finished size
43" × 65" (109 × 165 cm)

what you'll need

⅔ yd (61 cm) each of solid navy, cobalt, lime, and orange 45" (114.5 cm) wide quilting cotton for the quilt top

2 yd (1.8 m) of 60" (152.5 cm) wide quilting cotton or 3 yd (2.7 m) of 45" (114.5 cm) wide quilting cotton, pieced, for the backing

½ yd (45.5 cm) of 45" (114.5 cm) wide quilting cotton for the binding

72" × 90" (183 × 229 cm) twin-size quilt batting

Coordinating thread

Your sewing box

Rotary cutter, self-healing mat, and ruler

Handsewing needle (optional)

Quilting pins or basting spray (optional)

Quilter's binding clips (optional)

A home of one's own is like a dream come true. Celebrate someone's new home by giving a handmade quilt as a housewarming gift. The Dream Home Quilt is a lap-size quilt that's based on the width of quilting cotton fabric, which makes it straightforward to cut out. Depending on your skill set, free-motion quilt the word *dream* across the quilt horizontally or stick to simple straight-line stitching. The bold color and clean lines of the Dream Home Quilt will be a fresh and modern accent for any room.

prepare materials

Cut from the navy quilting cotton:

2 rectangles measuring 6" × 44" (15 × 112 cm) for the letter H

2 squares measuring 6" × 6" (15 × 15 cm) for the letter H and letter M

1 square measuring 6½" × 6½" (16.5 × 16.5 cm) for the letter M

2 squares measuring 7" × 7" (18 × 18 cm) for the letter M

1 rectangle measuring 6" × 22" (15 × 56 cm) for the letter M

Cut from the cobalt quilting cotton:

2 rectangles measuring 6" × 19¾" (15 × 50 cm) for the letter H

1 rectangle measuring 6" × 44" (15 × 112 cm) for the letter E

6 squares measuring 6" × 6" (15 × 15 cm) for the letter E

Cut from the lime quilting cotton:

2 rectangles measuring 6" × 44" (15 × 112 cm) for the letter O

2 squares measuring 6" × 6" (15 × 15 cm) for the letter O

4 rectangles measuring 6" × 14" (15 × 35.5 cm) for the letter E

Cut from the orange quilting cotton:

1 rectangle measuring 6" × 33" (15 × 84 cm) for the letter O

2 rectangles measuring 6" × 38½" (15 × 98 cm) for the letter M

1 square measuring 6" × 6" (15 × 15 cm) for the letter M

2 squares measuring 7" × 7" (18 × 18 cm) for the letter M

1 square measuring 6½" × 6½" (16.5 × 16.5 cm) for the letter M

Cut or piece from the backing fabric and the batting:

1 rectangle measuring 48" × 70" (122 × 178 cm)

Cut from the binding fabric:

5 rectangles measuring 2¼" (5.5 cm) × the width of the fabric

---

Piece the Letter H

1 With right sides facing, layer the 6" (15 cm) navy square onto the end of one 6" × 19¾" (15 × 50 cm) cobalt piece and sew together.

Layer the second 6" × 19¾" (15 × 50 cm) cobalt piece, right sides together, onto the navy square, aligning the raw edges, and sew. Press. This creates the center panel of the H.

2 Layer one 6" × 44" (15 × 112 cm) navy piece, right sides together, onto the sewn center panel of the H. Align the long edges and sew one set of edges together. Press.

Repeat, sewing the second 6" × 44" (15 × 112 cm) navy piece to the other long edge of the center H panel. Press.

Piece the Letter O

3 With right sides facing, layer one 6" (15 cm) lime square onto the end of the 6" × 33" (15 × 84 cm) orange piece. Sew the short edges together.

Layer the second 6" (15 cm) lime square, right sides together, onto the other end of the 6" × 33" (15 × 84 cm) orange piece, aligning the raw edges, and sew. Press. This creates the center panel of the O.

4 Layer one 6" × 44" (15 × 112 cm) lime piece, right sides together, onto the sewn center panel of the O. Align the long edges and sew one set of edges together. Press.

Repeat, sewing the second 6" × 44" (15 × 112 cm) lime piece to the other long edge of the center O panel, then press.

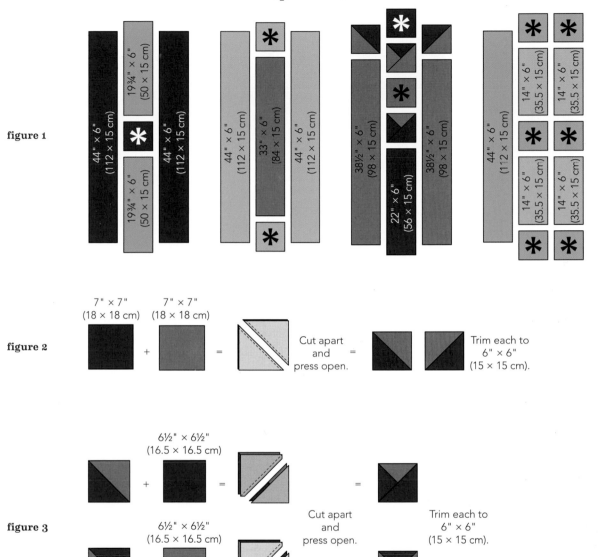

＊ = 6" × 6" (15 × 15 cm)

figure 1

44" × 6"
(112 × 15 cm)

19¾" × 6"
(50 × 15 cm)

19¾" × 6"
(50 × 15 cm)

44" × 6"
(112 × 15 cm)

44" × 6"
(112 × 15 cm)

33" × 6"
(84 × 15 cm)

44" × 6"
(112 × 15 cm)

38½" × 6"
(98 × 15 cm)

22" × 6"
(56 × 15 cm)

38½" × 6"
(98 × 15 cm)

44" × 6"
(112 × 15 cm)

14" × 6"
(35.5 × 15 cm)

14" × 6"
(35.5 × 15 cm)

14" × 6"
(35.5 × 15 cm)

14" × 6"
(35.5 × 15 cm)

figure 2

7" × 7"
(18 × 18 cm)

7" × 7"
(18 × 18 cm)

+   =   Cut apart
and
press open.

=   Trim each to
6" × 6"
(15 × 15 cm).

figure 3

6½" × 6½"
(16.5 × 16.5 cm)

+   =

=

6½" × 6½"
(16.5 × 16.5 cm)

+   =   Cut apart
and
press open.

=   Trim each to
6" × 6"
(15 × 15 cm).

Piece the Letter M

5 Layer a navy 7" (18 cm) square onto an orange 7" (18 cm) square, right sides together, and pin. Mark a diagonal line, corner to corner, with a pencil. Sew two seams, each ¼" (6 mm) from the line, and then cut along the line through both layers using a ruler and rotary cutter.

Press each pieced square open and trim evenly to 6" × 6" (15 × 15 cm) (**figure 2**, page 147). These will be the top outer points of the M.

6 Repeat this process using another navy 7" (18 cm) square and an orange 7" (18 cm) square, but trim both pieced squares to measure 6½" × 6½" (16.5 × 16.5 cm) instead of 6" (15 cm) square.

7 Following **figure 3** (page 147), layer a navy 6½" (16.5 cm) square, right sides together, on top of one of the pieced 6½" (16.5 cm) squares. Mark a diagonal line, corner to corner, opposite of the diagonal seam of the square underneath. Sew a seam on the line, and then cut ¼" (6 mm) below the line through all of the layers using a ruler and rotary cutter. Press and trim to measure 6" (15 cm) square. This will be the lower center point of the M.

8 Layer an orange 6½" (16.5 cm) square, right sides together, on top of the other 6½" (16.5 cm) pieced square. Mark a diagonal line, corner to corner, opposite the diagonal seam of the square underneath. Sew a seam on the line, then cut ¼" (6 mm) below the line through all layers using a ruler and rotary cutter. Press and trim to measure 6" (15 cm) square. This will be the upper center point of the M.

9 Referring to **figure 1** (page 147), layer one navy and orange square from Step 6, right sides together, on an orange 6" × 38½" (15 × 98 cm) piece, aligning the short edges. Sew and press the seam allowances down. This creates one leg of the M.

Repeat with the other navy and orange square from Step 6 and an orange 6" × 38½" (15 × 98 cm) piece to sew the other leg of the M.

10 To sew the center panel of the M, layer two adjacent squares at a time, right sides together, aligning the edges, and sew.

Layer the navy 6" × 22" (15 × 56 cm) rectangle onto the bottom square—the lower point of the M—right sides together and sew.

11 Layer the first leg of the M onto the center panel, right sides together. Take special care to align the intersecting seams precisely and to nest seam allowances. Sew the long edges together.

Repeat, sewing the second leg of the M to the other edge of the center panel.

Piece the Letter E

12 With right sides facing, layer one 6" (15 cm) cobalt square onto the end of one 6" × 14" (15 × 35.5 cm) lime piece and sew together.

Layer a second 6" (15 cm) cobalt square, right sides together, onto the other end of the 6" × 14" (15 × 35.5 cm) lime piece, aligning the raw edges, and sew.

13 Layer a second 6" × 14" (15 × 35.5 cm) lime piece on top of the second 6" (15 cm) cobalt square and sew with right sides together. Sew a third 6" (15 cm) cobalt square onto the end of the second 6" × 14" (15 × 35.5 cm) lime piece to complete the center panel of the E. Press all seam allowances in one direction.

Repeat to create the outer E panel. Press the seam allowances in the opposite direction of the center panel.

14 Layer the two panels, right sides together, matching the seams and nesting the seam allowances, then sew.

Layer the 6" × 44" (15 × 112 cm) cobalt piece on top of the center E panel and sew the long edges together. Press.

Assemble the Quilt Top

15 Referring to **figure 1**, layer the O onto the H, right sides together, and sew the long edge on the right-hand side. Open the seam and press.

16 Layer the M on top of the O, right sides together, and sew the long edge on the right-hand side. Open the seam and press.

17 Layer the E on top of the M, right sides together, and sew the long edge on the right-hand side. Open the seam and press.

18 Lay the quilt backing onto the floor, wrong side facing up. Layer the batting onto the quilt backing, smoothing out any wrinkles. Layer the quilt top, right side up, on top of the batting. Be sure to center the top so there are at least 2" (5 cm) of excess batting and backing on all sides.

Using hand-basting stitches, quilting pins, or basting spray, baste the quilt sandwich together.

19 Quilt the sandwich together by machine or by hand. If you're a beginning quilter, simple straight-line quilting would complement the striped layout.

If free-motion quilting is in your skill set, quilt the word "dream" in cursive, as shown. Take some time to practice your writing on some scraps before tackling the quilt. Start quilting from the center and work your way out toward the edges.

20 Trim the quilt to 43" × 65" (109 × 165 cm).

Bind the Quilt

21 Sew the cut binding pieces together by placing the ends of two pieces, right sides together, at a right angle. Sew diagonally at a 45-degree angle, from the top left corner to the bottom right corner, across the ends. Trim the excess ¼" (6 mm) from the seam. Press the seam allowances open.

Repeat this process to create one long binding strip from all of the pieces. (Refer to Techniques, page 154, for details on binding a quilt with mitered corners.)

22 Press the binding strip in half lengthwise, wrong sides together. Align one raw edge of the binding with the raw edges of the quilt top and pin. Leave a 5" (12.5 cm) tail of binding at the start. Sew the binding to the quilt sandwich, using a ¼" (6 mm) seam allowance.

23 As you stitch to each corner, fold the binding on the diagonal to miter. As you approach the starting tail of the binding, join the ends before sewing the last bit of binding to the quilt. Finish sewing the binding to the front of the quilt sandwich.

24 Press the binding away from the front. Fold the binding toward the backing and pin or secure with binding clips. Stitch in the ditch from the front, catching the binding on the back as you sew, or handstitch the binding to the back of your quilt.

sweet life
{ pillow }

finished size
16" × 16" (40.5 × 40.5 cm)

what you'll need

Sweet Life Pillow patterns on side D of the insert

½ yd (45.5 cm) of main fabric for the front borders and pillow back

⅓ yd (30.5 cm) of accent fabric for the hexagon pillow front

8½" × 11" (21.5 × 28 cm) piece of wool-blend felt for the bee

⅓ yd (30.5 cm) of fabric for the binding

½ yd (45.5 cm) of muslin

½ yd (45.5 cm) of batting

8½" × 11" (21.5 × 28 cm) sheet of fusible webbing

Coordinating thread

8½" × 11" (21.5 × 28 cm) sheet of self-adhesive water soluble stabilizer

18" (45.5 cm) square pillow form for a plump pillow

Your sewing box

Small embroidery scissors

Handsewing needle (optional)

Accent a friend's home with a beautiful handmade pillow. The Sweet Life Pillow features a honeybee motif made with reverse appliquéd felt. This special technique is easier than it looks because you stitch first, then trim away the felt to reveal the layers underneath. The body of the pillow is simply pieced and quilted and has a back envelope closure. This lively bee pillow will add a great buzz to any décor.

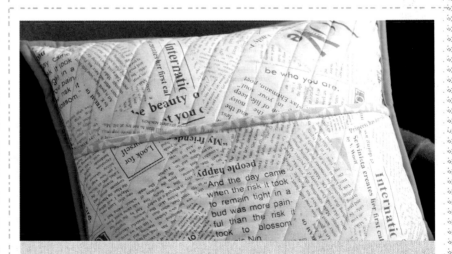

prepare materials

Cut from the main fabric:

2 strips measuring 3" × 13½"
(7.5 × 34.5 cm) for the side borders

2 strips measuring 2" × 16½" (5 × 42 cm)
for the top and bottom borders

1 rectangle measuring 8½" × 11"
(21.5 × 28 cm) for the appliqué

2 rectangles measuring 11" × 17"
(28 × 43 cm) for the envelope back

Using the pattern, cut from the main fabric:

2 Triangles

2 reversed Triangles

Using the pattern, cut from the accent fabric:

1 Hexagon

Cut from the muslin and the batting:

1 square measuring 17" × 17"
(43 × 43 cm) for the pillow front lining

2 rectangles measuring 11" × 17"
(28 × 43 cm) for the pillow back lining

Cut from the binding fabric:

2 strips measuring 2½" × 17" (6.5 ×
43 cm) for the envelope back binding

2 strips measuring 2½" (6.5 cm) × the
width of fabric for a total of at least 68"
(173 cm) for the outer binding

Cut from the felt:

1 rectangle measuring 8½" × 11"
(21.5 × 28 cm) for the bee

Create the Appliqué

1 Trace the Honeybee motif onto the right side of a sheet of self-adhesive water soluble stabilizer. Alternatively, scan the motif and print it directly onto the stabilizer sheet using an ink-jet printer.

2 Remove the paper backing and stick the sheet onto the right side of the 8½" × 11" (21.5 × 28 cm) felt rectangle. Layer the felt onto the right side of the 8½" × 11" (21.5 × 28 cm) appliqué rectangle. Pin together around the image area.

3 Sew through all layers with a straight stitch, following the outlines on the stabilizer.

At the end of a line, such as the leg or antenna, leave the needle down, lift the foot, and pivot the work. Continue stitching back over the previous stitch line. Keep stitching until every line has been stitched over at least once.

4 When the stitching is complete, soak the stitched felt and fabric in lukewarm water to dissolve the stabilizer. Gently press the fabric between towels to remove as much water as possible and let it air dry. Once dry, press with an iron.

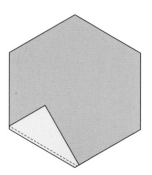

figure 1

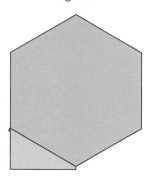

figure 2

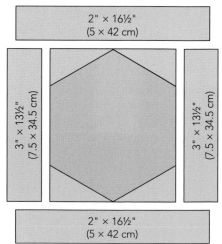

figure 3

Cut Away the Felt

5 With small embroidery scissors, snip through the felt layer only, ⅛" to ¼" (3 to 6 mm) from the stitching line inside the motif. Carefully follow the stitching line, trimming away areas of felt to reveal the appliqué fabric underneath.

6 Turn the work over so that the wrong side of the appliqué fabric is facing up. Place a piece of fusible webbing on top of the work with the webbing side down. Following the manufacturer's instructions, fuse the webbing to the back of the appliqué fabric, then turn the work over.

7 Trim away the felt, webbing, and fabric around the outside perimeter of the bee motif, cutting ⅛" to ¼" (3 to 6 mm) away from the stitching line. Trim around the legs and antennae. Peel off the paper backing.

Create the Pillow Front

8 With right sides together, place one Triangle piece onto the Hexagon piece, aligning the angled edges **(figure 1)**. Sew with a ¼" (6 mm) seam allowance. Press the seam allowances toward the triangle **(figure 2)**.

Repeat, sewing three more Triangles to the Hexagon. This is the center block of the pillow.

9 Sew side border pieces cut from the main fabric to the right and left sides of the pillow front. Sew the top and bottom border pieces to the top and bottom of the front **(figure 3)**. Press seams away from the hexagon.

10 Position the felt bee vertically onto the front, with the head and tail toward the top and bottom hexagon points. Cover with a press cloth and fuse it to the block.

Add more stitching to the appliqué if desired, following the previous stitch lines and further securing it to the pillow front.

11 Layer the pillow front, right side up, onto the 17" (43 cm) square of batting with the muslin on the bottom.

Baste together, then quilt. Keep stitching at least ¼" (6 mm) away from the appliqué. Trim the pillow front to a 16" (40.5 cm) square.

Sew the Pillow Back

12 Layer the 11" × 17" (28 × 43 cm) rectangles of backing, batting, and muslin to create two sets for the envelope back.

Baste and quilt each as desired. Trim the envelope back pieces to 10½" × 16" (26.5 × 40.5 cm).

13 Press an envelope back binding strip in half lengthwise, wrong sides together. Sew to the front long side of one back piece, right sides and raw edges together. Press the binding up and away from backing, then fold it to the muslin side and pin.

Stitch in the ditch from the front, catching the binding on the back as you sew (see Techniques, page 154).

Repeat with the remaining back piece.

Finish the Pillow

14 Lay the pillow front face down on the work surface. Place the pillow back rectangles on top of the pillow front, right sides up, aligning the raw edges on the top and bottom. The bound edges of the pillow back pieces will overlap in the middle, upper overlapping the lower.

Pin together around the perimeter of the pillow. Sew around all four sides using a seam allowance just under ¼" (6 mm).

15 Sew the two lengths of the outer binding strips together by placing an end from each, right sides together, at a right angle. Sew at a 45-degree angle, from the top left corner to the bottom right corner, across the ends. Trim the excess ¼" (6 mm) from the seam. Press the seam allowances open.

16 Press the sewn binding strip in half lengthwise, wrong sides together. Flip the pillow over and sew the binding to the pillow front, aligning the raw edges of the binding with the edge of the pillow, using a ¼" (6 mm) seam allowance.

17 As you stitch to each corner, fold the binding on the diagonal to miter. Press the binding away from the pillow. Fold the binding to the pillow back and pin. Stitch in the ditch from the front, catching the binding on the back as you sew, or handstitch the binding to the back of the quilt (see Techniques, page 154).

techniques

From embellishments to finishes, the details are what make your project come together with style and polish. The following techniques are provided to expand or sharpen your skills and to help you complete your project with confidence and satisfaction.

Stitching by Hand

A bit of embroidery will add an extra touch of beauty to your handmade gifts. These basic stitches are used in various projects throughout this book. Some of the techniques may be new to you, but you'll master them in no time with a bit of practice.

Backstitch

The backstitch is a great outline stitch because it makes a continuous line. Working the stitch from right to left, bring the needle up from the wrong side of the fabric on the stitching line at 1, insert it a short distance behind 1 at 2, bring the needle back up in front of 1 at 3, and pull the thread through (**figure 1**). Insert the needle again behind the stitch you just completed and come out a stitch length ahead of it.

Blanket stitch

A blanket stitch is a decorative stitch that can be used along the edge of a fabric or an appliqué. Work a blanket stitch from left to right, bringing the needle up at 1, stitch back down at 2, and come up again at 3, making sure the thread is under the needle (**figure 2**).

Pull on the thread to snug up the stitch, carefully aligning the thread loops along the edge of the fabric or appliqué, and continue stitching in this pattern across the entire edge.

Chain stitch

A chain stitch is a decorative embroidery stitch suitable for heavy outlines and borders. Bring the thread up through the fabric at 1. Insert the needle back in near 1 and poke it back up at 2, but don't pull the needle out completely. Put the thread around the needle to form a loop. Pull the needle through to tighten the loop to create the first link of the chain. Continue, putting the needle in near 2 (now inside the loop) and bring it out at 3 (outside of the loop). Continue the action to make the next loop of the chain (**figure 3**).

French knot

A French knot is a versatile stitch that's great for stuffed animal eyes and other embroidered accents. Bring the threaded needle up from the fabric's wrong side. Working close to the fabric, wrap the thread around

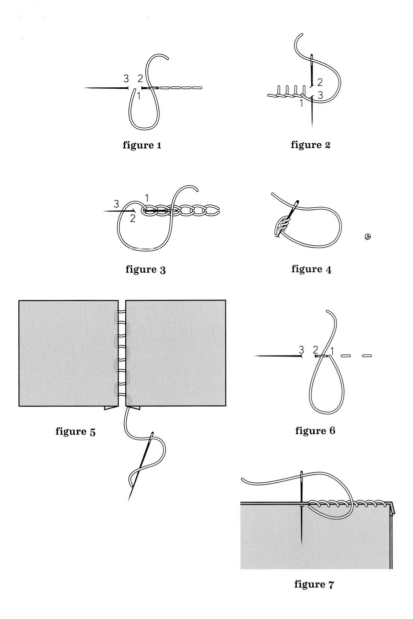

figure 1

figure 2

figure 3

figure 4

figure 5

figure 6

figure 7

Ladder stitch

The ladder stitch is ideal for closing stuffed objects. Fold the seam allowances under. Bring the threaded needle up through the folded edge. Insert the needle into the opposite fold and poke it out ⅛" to ¼" (3 mm to 6 mm) farther down the fold. Repeat until the seam is closed. Pull the stitches snug so the folded edges meet and the thread doesn't show **(figure 5)**.

Running stitch

To make this basic stitch, bring a threaded needle up from the wrong side of the fabric at 1, stitch back down at 2, and then come up again at 3 **(figure 6)**. Take stitches that are consistently about ⅛" (3 mm) long, and space the stitches the same length as the stitches themselves.

Whipstitch

A whipstitch is an overhand stitch generally used to join two finished edges. To whipstitch, bring the needle up from the wrong side of the fabric through one of the edges being joined **(figure 7)**. Insert the needle down in the second edge and bring it up again from the wrong side in the first edge. Continue inserting the needle from the fabric's back to front, taking small stitches to join the two edges.

Butted seam

A butted seam is a seam without a seam allowance, and it can be sewn either by hand or with your machine. Two pieces of fabric are placed side by side, touching but not overlapping, and are sewn together with a wide zigzag stitch.

If you're using a sewing machine, center your work under the machine needle and zigzag over the butted edges. If the edges pull apart as you sew, stop and readjust the work so the zigzag catches both edges evenly.

the needle two or three times. Holding the thread wraps in place near the needle's point, insert the needle back into the fabric close to, but not in, where the needle came up. Then pull the needle and thread out on the fabric's wrong side **(figure 4)**.

Secure the thread on the back of the fabric if you're making just one French knot, or bring the needle back up to the front of the fabric at the position of the next knot.

Clipping and Notching Seam Allowances

Curved seam allowances should be clipped on inner curves or notched on outer curves to allow the seam to lie flat and un-puckered when the sewn work is turned right side out. Use fabric scissors to make small snips in the seam allowance perpendicular to the stitching line, being careful not to clip into the stitches themselves **(figure 8)**. To notch a seam allowance, make angled clips into the allowance to remove small wedges of fabric **(figure 9)**.

Installing a Snap

Adding a magnetic snap to a bag or accessory is an easy way to give your project a secure, functional closure with a clean, professional look.

Following the indication on the pattern piece, mark the snap placement on the wrong side of the work. Fuse a small rectangle (about 1" × 2" [2.5 × 5 cm]) of fusible interfacing to the wrong side of the work, surrounding the snap placement area. This will provide reinforcement for the snap. Transfer the marking for the snap placement to the interfacing rectangle. Center the hole of one metal washer over the mark. Mark the interfacing inside the two rectangular prong holes with a pencil **(figure 10)**.

Set the washer aside and use a seam ripper to make a small slit through the interfacing and fabric on each prong mark. Realign the washer on the interfacing markings. From the right side of the fabric, push the prongs of the female snap component through the slits. With your fingers, bend the prongs down away from each other **(figure 11)**.

Repeat this procedure to install the male component of the snap to the appropriate project pieces.

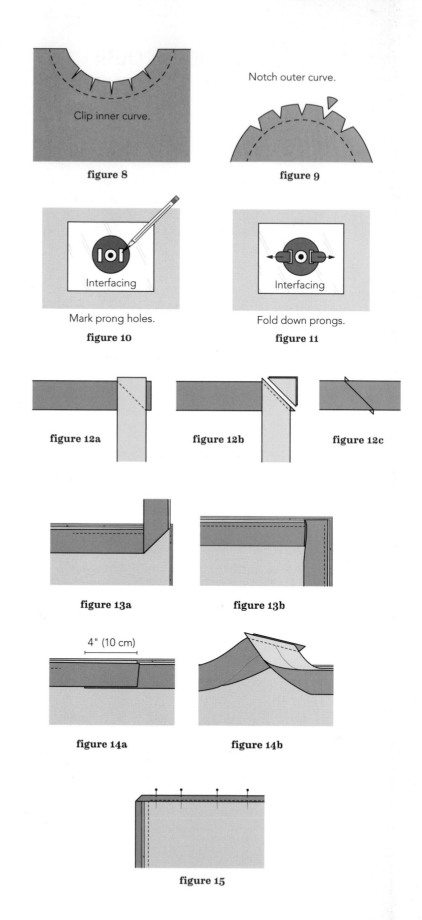

Clip inner curve.

figure 8

Notch outer curve.

figure 9

Mark prong holes.

Interfacing

figure 10

Fold down prongs.

Interfacing

figure 11

figure 12a

figure 12b

figure 12c

figure 13a

figure 13b

4" (10 cm)

figure 14a

figure 14b

figure 15

Binding a Quilt

There's more than one way to bind a quilt. There are also many opinions about which method is best. If you have a preferred method, whether it's bias or straight cut, machine or hand sewn, by all means do what's best for you. The following tips are provided to help you with some of the trickier parts of binding rather than quilting.

Joining binding strips

Once you've cut your binding strips following the project instructions, you'll need to seam them together into a longer continuous strip. Layer the ends of two strips, right sides together, at a right angle **(figure 12a)**. Sew at a 45-degree angle, diagonally from top left to bottom right, across the ends **(figure 12b)**. Trim the excess fabric ¼" (6 mm) away from the seam line and press the seam allowances open **(figure 12c)**. Repeat to join more strips as necessary.

Mitered corners

Starting about halfway between two corners, align the raw edges of one end of the folded binding with the raw edge of the quilt top, right sides together. Leave about 3" (7.5 cm) of binding free at the beginning, then pin several inches of binding to the quilt, toward its corner.

Begin sewing the quilt binding to the side of the quilt, using a ¼" (6 mm) seam allowance. Stop sewing before you reach the corner of the quilt, ending the seam ¼" (6 mm) from the approaching quilt edge. Backstitch, cut threads, and remove the quilt from the machine.

Fold the unsewn tail of quilt binding straight up, positioning it at a 90-degree angle from the newly sewn edge. The folded edge of the strip will form a 45-degree angle **(figure 13a)**.

Next, fold the binding down, aligning the top of the fold flush with the edge of the quilt top behind it and aligning its raw edge with the next side of the quilt **(figure 13b)**. The 45-degree angle should be intact under the fold. Pin the quilt binding to the side of the quilt, then sew the second side, ending ¼" (6 mm) from the next corner as before.

Miter the second corner as you did the first and continue sewing along the third side of the quilt. Miter the remaining corners in the same way.

Joining the ends

When you've sewn the binding to the last side, end the seam 4" to 6" (10 cm to 15 cm) from the original starting point and backstitch. Trim excess binding, leaving a tail that's long enough to overlap the first unsewn tail by about 4" (10 cm) **(figure 14a)**.

Unfold and make a 45-degree cut at the end of the beginning tail of quilt binding. Lay the unfolded ending tail under the angled beginning tail. Mark a line on the ending tail alongside the angled cut, then add a ½" (1.3 cm) seam allowance past the line and trim. Place the angled tails right sides together, offsetting their angled ends by ¼" (6 mm). Sew the binding ends together with a ¼" (6 mm) seam allowance **(figure 14b)**. Refold the quilt binding, then pin and sew the remainder to the quilt.

Stitch in the ditch

After the binding is sewn to the front of the quilt (or other project), fold the binding to the back of the quilt. Pin the binding to overlap the stitching line made when sewing the binding to the front. Using a bobbin thread that matches the binding and a top thread that blends well with the quilt top, stitch directly on top of the binding seam line—the ditch—on the quilt top. As you sew, your stitches will catch the outer edge of the binding at the back of the quilt **(figure 15)**.

resources

Conventional fabrics

Andover Fabrics
1384 Broadway, Ste. 1500
New York, NY 10018
andoverfabrics.com
Quilting cottons

Fairfield Fabrics
171 N. Pearl St.
Bridgeton, NJ 08302
fairfieldfabrics.com
Waxed canvas

National Nonwovens
P.O. Box 150
Easthampton, MA 01027
nationalnonwovens.com
100% wool felt and wool-blend felt

**Windham Fabrics/
Baum Textiles**
812 Jersey Ave.
Jersey City, NJ 07310
windhamfabrics.com
baumtextile.com
Quilting cottons

Organic cotton fabrics

Some of the following companies offer organic fabrics exclusively and some carry both organic and conventional cotton fabrics.

Alabama Chanin
462 Lane Dr.
Florence, AL 35630
alabamachanin.com
Organic cotton jersey

Birch Fabrics
1244 Pine St., Ste. D
Paso Robles, CA 93446
birchfabrics.com
Organic quilting cottons

Clothworks Textiles
6250 Stanley Ave. S.
Seattle, WA 98108
clothworks.com
Organic quilting cottons

Cloud9 Fabrics
335 Centennial Ave., Ste. 1
Cranford, NJ 07016
cloud9fabrics.com
Organic quilting cottons

Daisy Janie
1515 Dauphin Ave.
Wyomissing, PA 19610
daisyjanie.com
Organic quilting cottons

Free Spirit Fabrics
3430 Toringdon Wy., Ste. 301
Charlotte, NC 28277
freespiritfabric.com
Organic quilting cottons

Harmony Art
P.O. Box 892
Gualala, CA 95445
harmonyart.com
Organic quilting cottons

Michael Miller Fabrics
118 W. 22nd St., 5th Fl.
New York, NY 10011
michaelmillerfabrics.com
Organic cotton terry cloth

Monaluna
2367 Buena Vista Ave.
Walnut Creek, CA 94597
monaluna.com
Organic quilting cottons

Robert Kaufman
Box 59266, Greenmead Station
Los Angeles, CA 90059
robertkaufman.com
Organic quilting cottons

Spoonflower
2810 Meridian Pkwy., Ste. 176
Durham, NC 27713
spoonflower.com
Organic quilting cottons

Interfacings and stabilizers

ByAnnie
P.O. Box 1003
Saint George, UT 84771
byannie.com

Pellon Consumer Products
150 2nd Ave. N., Ste. 1400
St. Petersburg, FL 33701
pellonprojects.com

Therm-o-Web
770 Glenn Ave.
Wheeling, IL 60090
thermoweb.com

Bag hardware

Pacific Trimming
218 W. 38th St.
New York, NY 10018
pacifictrimming.com

Strapworks
3900 W. 1st Ave.
Eugene, OR 97402
strapworks.com

index

Enjoy even more *fun, colorful,* and *charming* projects

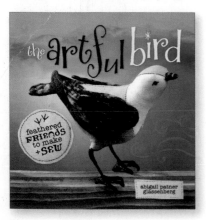